The Elder Sons of George III

To Mark, Anna, Madeline and Daniel,
with much love and very happy memories.

The Elder Sons of George III

Kings, Princes, and a Grand Old Duke

Catherine Curzon

PEN & SWORD HISTORY

First published in Great Britain in 2020 by
Pen & Sword History
An imprint of
Pen & Sword Books Ltd
Yorkshire – Philadelphia

ISBN 978 1 47387 247 9

A CIP catalogue record for this book is
available from the British Library.

Typeset by Mac Style
Printed and bound in the UK by TJ Books Ltd,
Padstow, Cornwall.

Pen & Sword Books Limited incorporates the imprints of Atlas,
Archaeology, Aviation, Discovery, Family History, Fiction, History,
Maritime, Military, Military Classics, Politics, Select, Transport,
True Crime, Air World, Frontline Publishing, Leo Cooper, Remember
When, Seaforth Publishing, The Praetorian Press, Wharncliffe
Local History, Wharncliffe Transport, Wharncliffe True Crime
and White Owl.

For a complete list of Pen & Sword titles please contact

PEN & SWORD BOOKS LIMITED
47 Church Street, Barnsley, South Yorkshire, S70 2AS, England
E-mail: enquiries@pen-and-sword.co.uk
Website: www.pen-and-sword.co.uk

Or

PEN AND SWORD BOOKS
1950 Lawrence Rd, Havertown, PA 19083, USA
E-mail: Uspen-and-sword@casematepublishers.com
Website: www.penandswordbooks.com

Contents

List of Illustrations

Acknowledgements

We're all used to this by now, but that doesn't make it any less important. My thanks are due to everyone at Pen & Sword, but particularly to Jon for the chips and consoles, and to the ever fierce and fabulous Lucy, my editor!

A wave of gratitude is sweeping towards everyone who has ever encouraged, cajoled or bullied me to keep on keeping on with these glorious Georgians. Extra big hugs go to Adrian, Rob, and Debra, for friendship, gin and for being there for the dreams that came true.

And, of course, cake, cuddles and the most massive hugs are reserved for Pippa, Nelly, and the Rakish Colonial – and UTT!

Introduction

'[My] actions shall ever be guided by the principle that my Sons are
the Instruments I look for assistance in putting this Country into
any degree of prosperity; but then they must by their behaviour
convince me they are deserving of such trust.'[1]

To King George III and his wife, Queen Charlotte of Mecklenburg-
Strelitz, there was little that they valued more in a person more than an
excellent character. Married for just shy of six decades and parted only
by Charlotte's death, the king and queen were faithful to each other for
the duration of their long union – in that, George was unique amongst
the four monarchs who shared his name.

George had been trained in the arts of sovereignty from an early age.
He was just 12 when his father, Frederick, Prince of Wales, died, and
from that day forward, he was sculpted into the very model of a British
sovereign. Not for him the German heritage of his predecessors, he
was devoted to all things English. Above all, he was devoted to what he
believed was his God-given duty.

The royal couple eschewed glitter and largesse in favour of simple family
values. They were parents to fifteen children - six girls and nine boys – and
an astonishing thirteen of their offspring lived to adulthood. The royal
children weren't always the strongest, but in a world where mortality
waited around every corner, to make it past infancy was no mean feat.

The girls drew the short straw when it came to growing up. Though
the eldest was lucky enough to marry and escape the royal household,
her sisters weren't so fortunate. For decades they remained at Windsor
as confidantes and secretaries to their bitter and domineering mother,
condemned to watch helplessly as their father's wits deserted him. In
contrast, the boys were allowed not only to glimpse freedom, but to
taste it.

Within reason.

George III was pious, fretful – some might even say repressed – and he expected his sons to follow in his fastidious footsteps. Yet such lofty expectations were all too easily disappointed. The sons of George III didn't want to shut themselves away and pursue respectability at all costs. Instead they craved excitement. In Georgian Britain that all too often meant scandal, debt and women.

Lots of women.

When I first conceived this book, I wasn't sure whether to include George IV. He is after all a man who has been written about extensively; indeed, I did so myself in my earlier book, *Kings of Georgian Britain*. But as the eldest son of George III, it didn't seem right not to include him here. *Prinny*, as George IV was known, isn't an easy man to ignore and without his presence, there would be a palpable hole in the narrative of the sons of George and Charlotte. For that reason, this behemoth of the monarchy has earned his place. His is a slightly more slender entry though – the only slender thing about him – which I hope will allow the stories of his brothers to truly flourish.

In these pages we'll meet the eldest sons of George III, from George to Edward via Frederick and William. We'll peek into the royal nursery and take a look at an unforgiving schoolroom before going on to meet the men who were forged there. There'll be secret marriages, illegitimate children, mistresses, gambling, and even attempted abduction. All royal life is here, and much of it will raise your eyebrows.

These are the men who emerged from the royal nursery to scandalise Britain and who ruled as kings, princes and a grand old duke.

The Royal Family

The marriage of George III and Queen Charlotte was what one might call *fruitful*. It was so fruitful, in fact, that it produced fifteen children. They're listed with their legitimate spouses below, but *legitimate* spouses were just the tip of the royal iceberg.

George IV (12 August 1762–26 June 1830)
Princess Caroline of Brunswick-Wolfenbüttel

Prince Frederick, Duke of York and Albany (16 August 1763–5 January 1827)
Princess Frederica of Prussia

William IV (21 August 1765–20 June 1837)
Princess Adelaide of Saxe-Meiningen

Charlotte, Princess Royal (29 September 1766–6 October 1828)
King Frederick of Württemberg

Prince Edward, Duke of Kent and Strathearn (2 November 1767–23 January 1820)
Princess Victoria of Saxe-Coburg-Saalfeld

Princess Augusta Sophia (8 November 1768–22 September 1840)
Princess Elizabeth (22 May 1770–10 January 1840)
Frederick, Landgrave of Hesse-Homburg

Ernest Augustus, King of Hanover (5 June 1771–18 November 1851)
Princess Friederike of Mecklenburg-Strelitz

Prince Augustus Frederick, Duke of Sussex (27 January 1773–21 April 1843)
Lady Cecilia Buggin

Prince Adolphus, Duke of Cambridge (24 February 1774–8 July 1850)
Princess Augusta of Hesse-Kassel

Princess Mary, Duchess of Gloucester and Edinburgh (25 April 1776–
30 April 1857)
Prince William Frederick, Duke of Gloucester and Edinburgh

Princess Sophia (3 November 1777–27 May 1848)
Prince Octavius (23 February 1779–3 May 1783)
Prince Alfred (22 September 1780–20 August 1782)
Princess Amelia (7 August 1783–2 November 1810)

Act One

A House of Sons

'You are now launching into a Scene of life, where You may either prove an honour, or a Disgrace to Your Family; it would be very unbecoming of the love I have for my Children, if I did not at this serious moment give You advice, how to conduct yourself; had I taken the common method of doing it in Conversation it would soon have been forgot: therefore I prefer this mode, as I trust You will frequently peruse this, as it is dictated from no other motive, than the anxious feelings of a Parent, that his Child may be happy, and deserve the approbation, of Men of worth and integrity.

It is highly necessary for every Rational Being, never to lose sight of the certainty, that every thought as well as action, is known to the All wise Disposer of the Universe; and that no solid comfort ever in this World can exist, without a firm reliance on His protection, and on His power to shield us from misfortunes: [...] therefore I strongly recommend the habitual reading of the Holy Scriptures, and Your more and more placing that reliance on the Divine Creator, which is the only real means of obtaining that peace of mind, that alone can fit a Man for arduous undertakings.

Remember You are now quitting home, where it has been the object of those who were placed about you to correct Your faults, yet keep them out of sight of the World; now You are entering into a Society [...] thus what would I hope have been cured, must now be instantly avoided, or will be for ever remembered to your disadvantage.'[1]

Do as I say, not as I do. Be pious. Be faithful. Trust God. Read the scriptures. Be everything I am and never, ever let me down.
Not too much of a tall order, eh?

King George III was a tough act to follow. Regardless of his politics or his personal life or his wobbly relationship with the colonies, one thing that can't be denied is the fact that he took his duty seriously. His father, Frederick, Prince of Wales, died as George was entering adolescence and the young man took his place in the line of succession. At 12-years-old, the boy who might reasonably have expected to have years to prepare for the throne found himself the heir apparent. King George II was nearly seventy at the time and wouldn't live forever.

When Frederick died, he left his son a set of instructions to follow that included advice on the economy, politics and all manner of other matters. Stick to these guidelines, wrote the late Prince of Wales, and 'I shall have no regret never to have worn the Crown, if you do but fill it worthily'[2]. It was a sentiment that George III took deeply to heart in his quest to honour his father's memory and serve his country. His sons were not quite so keen to play by the rules.

Happy Ever After

George III succeeded to the throne of the United Kingdom in 1760 at the age of 22. He was unmarried and therefore had no heirs, something that Parliament was keen to put right as soon as possible. It set to work on compiling a list of possible brides for the new king and every name on it was that of a respectable Protestant lady of childbearing age and suitable birth. Yet George wasn't impressed by the candidates and sent the list back for revisions. One of those revisions was the addition of Charlotte of Mecklenburg-Strelitz, a young lady of relatively little note from an inconsequential kingdom.

The king received the new list and something about Charlotte caught his eye. It wasn't exactly love at first sight, more like the best of an unremarkable bunch, but George decided that she was the queen for him. The couple were wed on 8 September 1761. It was the start of nearly six eventful decades of marriage.

The First Sons

'At seven this morning her Majesty was safely delivered of a Prince at the palace of St. James's to the great joy of his Majesty and of all his loyal subjects, who consider the birth of this heir to the crown as a pledge of the future felicity of their posterity under the happy auspice of his royal family.

[...]

It is worthy observation, that her Majesty is brought to-bed of an heir to the crown on the same day that our most gracious Sovereign's great grand-father, King George the first, succeeded to the crown of these kingdoms.'[3]

The heir to the throne had arrived, born to his first-time mother who was only 18 at the time, and had endured an unforgiving labour. In one fell swoop, Charlotte had gone halfway to fulfilling her duty. She had given birth to the heir, now there was only the spare to go. In fact, over the years that followed, she would give birth to no less than eight more sons, leaving plenty of spares to go around.

The childhood of a prince was one of constant attendance from a retinue of staff, from cradle rockers to wet nurses, who all served under the watchful eye of Lady Charlotte Finch, the faithful and long-serving governess. For those entrusted with his care, George, the little Prince of Wales, would prove to be intelligent, wilful and precocious. It was to become a heady and dangerous mix as he grew into adulthood.

The royal sons each took their turn to be on public display after their births and illustrious members of society made a pilgrimage to pay tribute beside their cradles. Public celebrations were held to mark the occasion and as the cannons were fired and the people of London flocked to St James's to enjoy a piece of cake and a cup of the eggnog-like caudle, the mood was always one of triumphant joy.

Each son that came along was subjected to a rigorous education programme, beginning with the Prince of Wales and his brother and best friend, Frederick, the future Duke of York, who was born almost exactly a year to the day after George. The intellectual development of the boys was entrusted to Lord Holderness – Horace Walpole's 'solemn phantom' - and a handpicked team of carefully selected tutors, with nothing left to chance. The hours were long and the discipline tough. Good behaviour, dedication and piety were the order of the day and should there be any bad behaviour, it was punished swiftly and sharply. Not a minute went by that wasn't accounted for and the king and queen constantly watched their sons, determined that they would be made into the very model of decent young men. Meals were humble and the young princes were given the chance for physical improvement by tending their own little agricultural plots, reflecting the king's love of the simple life that earned him the nickname, *Farmer George*. It was a far from decadent childhood.

When the king and queen weren't watching their sons, they were at pains to remind the children that the Almighty *was*. Just after the little prince turned eight, Queen Charlotte wrote to her son to 'recommend Unto You to fear God' and to entreat him to show 'the highest Love, affection and Duty towards the King. Look upon him as a Friend: nay as the greatest, the best and the most deserving of all Friends You can possibly find. Try to imitate his virtues and look upon every thing that is in Opposition to that Duty, as destructive to Yourself.'[4] At eight years old it was difficult enough, but as the years passed it would prove to be impossible.

Should the boys step out of line they were 'flogged like dogs with a long whip'[5] by their tutors, but even this failed to mould them into replicas of their pious father. As you'll learn, both Wales and York later rebelled against this treatment in fine style. When Charlotte advised the little boy to 'Disdain all Flatery [sic]: it will corrupt Your manners, and render You Contemptible before the World,'[6] she might as well have told him to hold back the tide. The Prince of Wales loved flattery above all things.

Other than women and spending money, that is.

As the youngest boys grew, so too did the king's political headaches. Though he had yet to fall into madness, his nerves were a constant strain. He relaxed in the garden or by joining the family for occasional trips to the theatre. Cultural enrichment was important if strictly controlled, but education was the focus of the young princes' lives just as it had once been for the adolescent George III.

When ill health forced Lord Holderness to give up his position in 1775, he was replaced by Richard Hurd, Bishop of Lichfield and Coventry, and the educational regime continued apace. The routine was set and unwavering, beginning at 7.00 am and continuing until dinner at 3.00 pm, after which there were more lessons and reading. Every royal child, whether boy or girl, was slotted neatly into an educational regime that was dedicated to turning out perfect princes and princesses like a production line. It was working, George and Charlotte decided, so there was no reason to change it.

The first batch of royal sons came along at regular intervals. First came the Prince of Wales, then the Duke of York. The future William IV was born in 1765, followed in 1767 by Edward, who was one day to be Duke of Kent and Strathearn. Queen Charlotte took a break then, not from children but from boys. For the first twenty years of her marriage she was almost constantly pregnant or recovering from childbirth. It must have been exhausting.

The Middle Children

With Edward's birth, the royal children now numbered five. His siblings were George, Frederick, William and their sister, Charlotte, Princess Royal. The king and queen were keen to have not only a large family – a particular ambition of the king's – but a good mix of boys and girls too. Charlotte's next two pregnancies did much to balance the scales and a pair of daughters were born to the royal family followed by Ernest Augustus in 1771, who would later reign as King of Hanover. Ernest's birth completed the trio of future sovereigns, but it didn't complete the family tree. In fact, Charlotte was back on schedule and in 1773 and 1774 she delivered Augustus Frederick and Adolphus, respectively the Dukes of Sussex and Cambridge.

For this trio, life was much as it had been for their elder brothers. They were schooled by their tutors and moved around the various homes of their parents as the seasons and draughty corridors dictated. The king tried to avoid spending too much time in London and far preferred the seclusion of Kew, where Ernest, Augustus and Adolphus lived in a cottage with their tutors. Sadly, Kew would eventually be forever tarnished for

George III after he was confined there by the doctors who treated him during his periods of madness.

Whilst Charlotte kept a hawk-like watch on her daughters, George was happy to assume the role of good cop. Beset by challenges in government and the overseas colonies, he loved to lose himself in a few hours spent with the younger children and was a more than willing playmate for them. Each evening, the youngest were brought to the king's rooms and there George indulged and entertained them until bedtime, winding down from the cares of the day. Charlotte followed a much stricter approach to parenting, regardless of the age or gender of the child. She had even been known to reproach her husband when he crawled about on his hands and knees, chasing the youngest of the brood across the rugs. Yet as the younger boys enjoyed playtime, their elder brothers were spending longer hours than ever in the schoolroom. George III might be a doting father, but he wasn't about to let his sons forget that one day they would have a duty to represent the family name.

Following the early death of his own father, the king had been raised in a secluded world. He had precious few playmates of his own age and any adult he encountered was carefully vetted to ensure that they were suitable company. It was an approach George applied to his own children too, though thankfully they had plenty of siblings to socialise with. George and Charlotte were convinced that their approach would pay dividends and turn their sons, particularly the heir to the throne, into serious-minded, pious and dutiful men, who would avoid scandal and impropriety just as their mother and father had done.

As we'll see, things didn't quite go that way.

A Turbulent Life

George III was devoted to his family and the uncomplicated company of his children was a tonic to him through his most troubled years. Whilst the girls were cocooned in cotton wool and kept away from society, the boys were being prepared for a life in the service of their country. Dedication to the realm was something that their father knew all too much about and anxiety over sabre rattling in the colonies was to lead to his first serious bout of ill health, which took the form of a violent cold and a stitch. Over the years, physical pains would serve as a warning of a forthcoming breakdown for the unfortunate monarch.

It wasn't only politics and colonists that caused the king headaches either. George and Charlotte had enjoyed a happy marriage which meant, as far as they were concerned, that dynastic unions were the way forward for their children too. These future marriages were a source of worry to the king, and this anxiety had begun years earlier with one of his more wayward siblings.

In 1769 George III's brother, Prince Henry, Duke of Cumberland, was sued for adultery by Lord Grosvenor. The prince had been caught having a torrid affair with Lady Grosvenor and when it was dragged into court, the case seemed like something out of a *Carry On* film. Cumberland had employed pseudonyms, disguises and comical fake accents in order to enjoy secret assignations with his paramour and Grosvenor, who was far from pure himself, was determined to make him pay. Grosvenor won the case and Cumberland was landed with a bill for damages totalling £10,000. He turned to the king, cap in hand, and the king turned to Parliament, who had no choice but to buy off the cuckolded Lord Grosvenor.

George hoped that Cumberland had learned his lesson, but he was wrong. Two years later, Cumberland sprang a fresh surprise on his brother when he handed him a letter as they strolled at Richmond Lodge. The letter contained a confession from Cumberland that he had secretly married a widowed commoner named Anne Horton. He begged the king for his blessing but for George, it was a step too far. He banished Cumberland from his presence, causing an estrangement that went on for years.

So enraged was the sovereign at his brother's subterfuge that he became obsessed with ensuring that it could never happen again. With Charlotte's support he pursued a new Royal Marriages Act that would forever put an end to such unsuitable marriages. He turned to his brother, Prince William Henry, Duke of Gloucester and Edinburgh, for a shoulder to lean on and Gloucester provided just that. What he *didn't* provide was the pertinent information that he was husband to a clandestine wife himself.

In 1766 Gloucester had married Maria Walpole, the widowed Countess Waldegrave. Maria was from wealthy stock but despite being deeply in love, her parents had never got around to tying the knot. It didn't matter how much money she had, she was still illegitimate. Had Gloucester asked George for his blessing to wed Maria, he would never have received it. Besides, he didn't have to ask permission, but it would have been good manners to do so.

Blissfully unaware of Gloucester's deceit, George decided that the only way to prevent another such embarrassment was legislation. With the assistance of prime minister, Lord North, he pushed the Royal Marriages Act through a reluctant Parliament.

The new act ruled that any descendants of George II must in future request and receive the permission of the monarch before they could marry. If permission was withheld from a member of the royal family aged over 25, they could give notice of the intended marriage to the Privy Council instead. On the condition that they waited a year and neither the House of Commons nor the House of Lords objected, then the wedding could go ahead. If a wedding was undertaken without following the provisions of the Act, it would be void, and any children from the marriage would be ruled illegitimate and removed from the line of succession. The Act proved controversial amongst the public, who recoiled from it as the action of a tyrannical king hoping to strangle the independence of his siblings. Nevertheless, George wouldn't be dissuaded. Though Cumberland came to the House of Lords to speak against it, the Royal Marriages Act was given the Royal Assent on 1 April 1772, just two months after the death of the king's beloved – some might say domineering – mother, the Dowager Princess of Wales.

Only months later did George discover that the act had come too late for one of his brothers. With Maria pregnant, the Duke of Gloucester finally confessed to the king that he and his constant companion were more than simply lovers. George III ordered his brother to choose between brotherly love or his secret bride. Gloucester chose Maria and, just like Cumberland before him, he too was banished.

And all this *before* George III lost America. It wasn't an easy time.

The Youngest

By the time the Prince of Wales came of age, one might be forgiven for assuming that Queen Charlotte's childbearing days were over. If so, one would be mistaken, because she was far from done with childbirth.

Charlotte gave birth to the last of her children in quick succession, with the arrival of Octavius in 1779 and Alfred just over eighteen months later. She rounded off her brood with Princess Amelia in 1783, meaning there was almost twenty-one years between the births of her eldest and youngest children. The last three babies born to Charlotte and George were blighted by ill health and for two of them, their years would be short indeed. Princess Amelia did manage to reach adulthood, but her death in 1810 would rock the king's sanity to its core.

For every child, the expectations were the same. Duty, piety and obedience were everything. And yet, despite the concerted efforts of their parents and tutors, the sons of George III and Charlotte of Mecklenburg-Strelitz lived lives that were anything *but* devoted to piety and protocol. In fact, it sometimes seemed as if they went out of their way to do precisely the opposite.

Act Two

George IV (12 August 1762–26 June 1830)

A Lover, Not a Fighter

'Yesterday morning, at twenty-four minutes after seven o'clock, her Majesty was brought to bed of a Prince, after being in labour somewhat above two hours.

[…]

The Prince is born Duke of Cornwall, and according to custom, will, we suppose, soon be created Prince of Wales, and Earl of Chester.

It is something remarkable, that his Royal Highness was born on the anniversary of his illustrious family's accession to the imperial throne of these kingdoms, and about the hour of the day on which that succession took place.'[1]

Generally, when a child is raised as George, Prince of Wales was, it can go one of two ways. The stern education, regular beatings and unflinching focus on propriety will either create a son who is exactly what his parents had hoped for, or the son in question will push back against his upbringing and forge his own path, for better or worse. After eighteen years of plain food and harsh discipline, the Prince of Wales famously took the latter option. He had been told that the eye of the Almighty was on him, but George was more interested in the eyes of society.

As the prince grew up in the company of his best friend and brother, the Duke of York, and their unforgiving tutors, his mind wasn't on the crown, but the army. He had a lifelong fascination with the military and dreamed of a career spent in the defence of his country, but it wasn't to be. No king-in-waiting could risk his life on the battlefield, no matter how much he begged, so instead the prince was eventually appointed Colonel of the 10th (Prince of Wales's Own) Regiment of (Light) Dragoons, who were famed for their fashionable uniforms and wealthy officers. Indeed, Beau Brummell himself was a member of the regiment until it did the unthinkable and relocated to Manchester.

Denied a military career, George needed something else to occupy his gadfly mind and for a bright, pretty prince with a love of the high life that had always been denied him, there was only one thing for it.

Women.

Whether as Prince of Wales, Prince Regent or King George IV, George *loved* women and was never without at least one mistress. That's before we even consider his wives – both of them! To include every lover of this noted Casanova would need an encyclopaedia, so we'll content ourselves with the most notable, not to mention the most scandalous.

George had a romantic heart and whenever he fell for a woman, he fell hard. The pattern was set early in life when he developed an attachment to Mary Hamilton, one of the ladies who attended his sisters. George was just 16 at the time and Mary was in her early twenties, but he didn't let that stop him. He bombarded her with love letters and locks of his hair, but she was quick to dissuade him of his romantic ideas. A wise move given the cavalcade of lovers that would follow.

Many a Georgian discovered his paramour at the theatre and George was no exception. Though his upbringing was austere, theatre was one of the few pleasures he could indulge and at the age of 17 he accompanied his mother and father to a royal command performance of *The Winter's Tale*. In the leading role of the dreamy Perdita was Mary Darby Robinson, a celebrated comedienne whose life to date had been every bit as eventful as her stage roles. She'd survived smallpox and even a stay in debtor's prison as a result of her no-mark husband, but Mary's life was now one of triumph and what could be more triumphant than snagging the heir to the throne?

Or so she thought.

George was determined to charm his way into Mary's life and their mutual friend, Lord Malden, was more than happy to do what was necessary to make the path of true love – or at least passion – run smoothly. Mary was already a star so when the Georgian paparazzi got wind of the prince's interest and especially the irresistible fact that his love letters to Mary were written from *Prince Florizel* to *Perdita*, they went to town.

'Last winter a certain Nobleman, well known for his attachment to the fair *Perdita*, in order to ingratiate himself with the *Rising Sun*, and advance the fortune of his beloved, proposed to *Perdita* to dress herself in the most captivating stile [sic], and sit in the opposite box to *Florizel*, at the Oratorio at Drury-Lane Theatre, and she would undoubtedly make a complete conquest of his youthful heart, as he had already spoken of her in the most partial manner to several Noblemen, on seeing her perform on the Stage.

The bait took: *Florizel's* eyes were so rivetted on the charms of our heroine, that numbers of the spectators took immediate notice of it: nay, it did not even pass unnoticed by the *Mother of Florizel*, who sent a messenger to the Manager, desiring the Lady to remove from that box, which he obeyed, but all to no purpose; *Perdita* alledging [sic], that as She had paid *that night* for her seat, which was really the case, She had a right to sit in that box, the place being kept for her by her servant.

Next day *Florizel* sent an epistle to *Perdita*, by Lord [Malden]; and the Lady came to an immediate capitulation.'[2]

So, Mary had resisted the entreaties of the Queen herself to give up her seat and keep out of sight of the easily charmed prince. Yet to say that she capitulated immediately is an over-simplification. In fact, Mary drove a hard bargain, aware of the rewards that awaited her as the mistress of the prince and determined to wring the best deal she could out of him. Meetings were brief and chaperoned by Lord Malden or the Duke of York, but George was determined to win her over and make her his. Eventually the prince hit on a winning formula and invited Mary to be his mistress on condition that she give up her errant husband, abandon her career and accept a payment of £20,000 to compensate her for her troubles. Mary said yes. In doing so, she became the first woman to discover that the only ladies the Prince of Wales really wanted were those that he couldn't have.

When he hit 18, the Prince of Wales moved into his own establishment at Carlton House, where he immediately commissioned a programme of expensive renovations. Here he could gamble, drink and womanise to his heart's content. Suddenly, Mary was in the way. George gave her the elbow *before* she'd received her £20,000. Mary was furious and humiliated, her ruin and embarrassment crowed over by the salivating press. But Mary had seen it all in her relatively short life and she wasn't about to go without a fight. She threatened to sell the prince's love letters to the highest bidder unless he bought her silence with a lump sum of £25,000.

George was having none of it. Eventually his abandoned paramour was paid off with a relatively meagre £5,000 and the promise of £500 per year for life. It was like getting blood from a stone.

And George? He was too busy living the high life to care.

Love and Money

One of the lasting legacies of George's relationship with Mary Robinson was a passionate interest in politics. Unfortunately for the Tory George III, his son's sympathies lay with the Whigs, and one of his closest friends was Charles James Fox, a prominent Whig politician with whom the Prince of Wales shared some of his lovers, as well as his politics.

Fox's considerable influence in Parliament was useful for George and having the heir to the throne as a friend was a gift for the ambitious politician, so between them they made quite a pair. George was quick to make the best of his friend's connections and when the king refused to settle his mounting debts, the prince turned to Fox for help. It was the wily Fox who negotiated George's move to Carlton House, as well as a healthy allowance to keep the young royal afloat.

Cash – spending it, lacking it, begging for it – was a constant theme of George's life. The other constant was women and for the Prince of Wales, there were *dozens* of them. He went through lovers at a rate of knots but one in particular was to remain forever the one that got away. Or the one that George pushed away.

Maria Fitzherbert was a Roman Catholic who had been unlucky in love. Twice married, her first marriage had ended in tragedy when her husband was killed falling from a horse just three months after he said, *I do*. Though he was a wealthy man, he left no will and poor Maria found herself with nothing. Her second husband fared a little better and lived for three years after the wedding. When he passed away, he left his fortune to Maria Fitzherbert.

Maria was six years older than the Prince of Wales and she had seen enough of life to know that he had a reputation for loving ladies and leaving them. Mrs Fitzherbert wasn't about to be the next to face that sorry fate. Instead, she played hard to get and the more she spurned his advances, the more determined George became. The couple shared a mutual society friend, Georgiana, Duchess of Devonshire, and when the prince realised that his Roman Catholic paramour wasn't going to capitulate unless he pulled a blinder, it was the unwitting Duchess who he roped into the pantomime.

And what a show he was about to give.

In 1784, George sent word to Maria that he simply couldn't live without her. In despair at her continued rejection of his advances, he had attempted suicide and stabbed himself almost fatally. Or so he said. The Prince of Wales never did anything subtle, but the thought of him genuinely taking his own life is just too silly to contemplate. He was far too fond of living for that. Instead he had conceived a piece of theatre designed to bring Maria running, and naturally it worked like a charm.

With the Duchess of Devonshire as her chaperone, Maria raced to Carlton House. She found the prince in bed, wrapped in bloodstained bandages and lingering on the edge of oblivion. The time for goodbyes had come, he told her weakly, and his dying wish was only that Maria would accept a token of his esteem before he slipped away forever. Maria said that she would, and George asked Georgiana if he might borrow her ring. Despite her better judgement, the duchess agreed, and George slipped the ring onto Maria's finger.

And just like that, he declared himself not only cured, but betrothed. As George tore off his bandages, Maria realised that she'd been duped. She threw the ring back and fled, taking off for Europe and leaving the Duchess of Devonshire to sign a statement in which she confirmed that there was no betrothal, only a con trick designed to ensnare an innocent woman. George immediately asked his father for permission to travel to the continent, claiming that he wished to move abroad in order to live more cheaply. The king saw through his ruse straight away and told his son that there was to be no trip to Europe. Instead, George was to remain in England, far away from the woman he adored.

Though the 1701 Act of Settlement ruled that marrying a Catholic would result in an heir being removed from the line of succession, George pursued Maria until she gave in. She returned to England in 1785 and the couple were married in a secret ceremony at her house in Mayfair. As a Roman Catholic, there was no way George would have received his father's permission to marry Maria, so he went ahead and did it without asking, meaning that the marriage was void. To him, the Royal Marriages Act wasn't worth the paper it was written on.

The press, of course, knew nothing of the wedding even as they devoted miles of newsprint to the suddenly very interesting adventures of Maria Fitzherbert. Her every move was watched and when journalists thought it worth reporting that 'Mrs Fitzherbert was in the Royal box'[3], everybody knew what that meant. Mrs Fitzherbert was in the royal bed too, so much a fixture that Prince William sent 'My best compliments to M'[4] when he wrote to his brother the year after the secret wedding. By then Maria had become familiar with several of the princes, although none of them attended the marriage, or indeed, knew anything about it. Still, she was well-known to George's bothers, so much so that half a decade later, Prince Edward told Wales, 'allow me to offer my best and most sincerely affectionate compliments to Mrs Fitzherbert.' The secret was only a secret for those who preferred to turn a blind eye. To everyone else, George and Maria were soon the subject of all sorts of rumours for 'what other inference could the public draw from [her closeness to the prince] than that she was actually the princess of Wales?' asked *The Times*. 'This matter will soon be ascertained.'[5]

The couple went everywhere together and soon became the most fashionable twosome in the land. To the world at large, they were prince and mistress, but Maria and George knew that they were husband and wife. For a little while he was content, but eventually he grew restless. After all, what good was a wife when the land was full of willing young ladies, all of whom wanted a chance with the pretty prince? Maria had to go.

Events and finances had overtaken George once more and society rumours regarding his relationship with the widow Fitzherbert were getting louder and louder. Eventually whispers of a secret wedding reached the king and when the prince went to him to request a financial bailout for his latest gambling debts, George III said no. The Prince of Wales turned instead to his friend Fox and told him to issue a public denial that there had been any clandestine wedding. He'd discussed none of this with Maria so the last thing she expected to hear was that her private life had been discussed at Westminster. When Fox stood up in the House of Commons and declared categorically that 'his Highness was not married to Mrs. Fitzherbert, as had been affirmed in a pamphlet,'[6] she was heartbroken.

The upshot of all this was that George got the money he wanted, amounting to a cool £150,000 fortune and certainly enough to finance his lifestyle at Carlton House for a while. The Prince of Wales no longer needed Maria. He moved out of her home on Park Street with indecent haste, leaving her high, dry and humiliated.

The Regent-in-Waiting

George and Maria were over – mostly – but the prince's relationship with his parents was far from steady. They had hoped to raise a son in their own image but instead they had a profligate, flighty ladies' man with a taste for the most expensive things in life. Unlike his brothers, the Prince of Wales had been denied the chance to serve his country due to his status as heir to the throne, but he had plenty of other ways to fill his time. What he had reckoned without as he gadded through London and Brighton society was the frail health of his father.

George might have reasonably expected to have years to go before he had to even think about ruling the country but if that was the case, he was to be sorely mistaken. In 1788 George III complained of a violent and prolonged stomach ache, but what began with physical symptoms soon proved to be the first signs of something far more worrying. At first the king's physicians encouraged him to take the waters at Cheltenham Spa, but this malady was far beyond anything that healing waters could cure. By the time he returned to Kew in the autumn, George was in dire straits.

The king's wits appeared to have entirely deserted him. He ranted and gabbled for hours on end, foaming at the mouth and constantly on edge. His usually reserved temperament became violent and he barely slept a wink. In despair at her husband's worsening condition, Queen Charlotte placed him in the care of Dr Francis Willis, a Lincolnshire clergyman turned physician who had been credited with restoring the mental health of a distressed courtier. Willis' methods were brutal by modern standards but in the world of the eighteenth century, they were par for the course, forward thinking even. Over the years of his regime, Willis had the king's head shaven and blistered, held him in a straitjacket and refused to show him any deference at all. When his methods eventually appeared to pay dividends and the king was restored to health, Willis became one of the most sought-after physicians in the land.

It was an audacious way to treat a monarch and when the ailing sovereign joined his family for dinner one evening in late 1788, his appearance shocked them to the core. His legs were swollen and bandaged, his eyes bulged in his skull and his head was shaved. The tottering king carried his weight on a walking cane and as the meal progressed, he talked without pause or reason. At the end of the meal, to the horror of his wife and daughters, George dragged the Prince of Wales from his seat and hurled him bodily across the room. This, said the men in Westminster, was not a person who should be left in charge of a country. A regent must be appointed in the interests of the 'Peace & Happiness of the Royal Family [and] the Safety & Welfare of the Nation.'[7]

In terms of simplicity, the obvious candidate to serve as Prince Regent was the Prince of Wales, the heir to the throne. Yet in Parliament, obvious didn't necessarily mean most popular. The Whig opposition was rather keen on having its royal cheerleader in such an exalted position, ready to dispense whatever favours he saw fit. George III's favoured Tories, quite naturally, were not. As both sides of the House battled it out, prime minister William Pitt the Younger drew up a Regency Bill designed to enshrine not only the name of the Regent in law, but their rights and responsibilities too. At the same time, Fox was lobbying hard for his friend to get the top job. Fearing that Fox would be installed as prime minister in his place if the Prince of Wales became regent, Pitt had other ideas. The press knew it too.

'The matter of the Regency, is whispered in the circle of fashion to be thus settled […] The point of the Regency is within a narrow compass of dispute – it is, shall CHARLES FOX or WILLIAM

PITT be Minister? Fifteen sixteenths of the subjects of Great
Britain are in favour of the latter Gentleman – His MAJESTY was
of the same opinion, and a large majority of the House of Commons
confirmed that matter.' [8]

As they battled it out, George waited on the sidelines to see if and when
he would take control of his father's realm. This time the cards weren't
in his favour. The politicians argued back and forth for so long that
eventually the ailing king turned the corner and began to recover. For his
eldest son, that meant a return to partying. And falling back into the arms
of Mrs Fitzherbert.

A Married Man

As the Regency crisis passed, the Prince of Wales and Maria Fitzherbert
were together once again. They lived it up on the south coast at Brighton,
becoming the unofficial king and queen of an alternative court where the
most fashionable people in the land congregated, but their idyll couldn't
last. Just like all the ladies in his life, once Maria capitulated to George's
attentions, her days were numbered. She was no match for the glamorous
and intriguing Frances Villiers, Countess of Jersey, and when she became
the prince's lover in 1793, Lady Jersey was determined to remove Maria
from the equation once and for all. She knew that George really did love
his clandestine wife and as long as Maria was on the scene, she'd never
quite be number one.

Perhaps surprisingly, her answer was another wedding.

As wife of the 4th Earl of Jersey, the capricious and manipulative Lady
Jersey was off the market. There were plenty of other eligible women
available though and the king and queen were keen to find their wayward
eldest son a bride and get him settled. Their favoured candidate was his
cousin, Caroline of Brunswick, and his parents promised the perennially
cash-strapped prince a financial sweetener should he say yes. George
wasn't keen on the idea of marriage, but the conniving Lady Jersey
convinced him to go along with the plan. She knew that Caroline was
far less competition for the affections of the Prince of Wales than Maria
was. Even better, George was happy to install Lady Jersey as Caroline's

Lady of the Bedchamber, meaning his mistress was perfectly positioned to sabotage, gossip and connive.

> 'I have also much satisfaction in announcing to you that I have concluded a treaty for the marriage of my son, the Prince of Wales, with the Princess Caroline, the daughter of the Duke of Brunswick. The uniform expression of affection, which I have experienced from my people to my person and family, convinces me that they will be pleased with this addition to my domestic happiness, and that a provision for their establishment will be made suitable to the rank of the Heir Apparent of my Crown.'[9]

When the marriage was announced to Parliament in the king's speech, it spelled the end for George and Maria but the beginning of one of the messiest affairs that British royalty had ever seen. The optimistic king hoped that love – or duty – would conquer all and wrote to his son to express his wish that the marriage might 'prove so pleasing to you that your mind may be engrossed with domestic felicity, which may establish in you that composure of mind perhaps the most essential qualification in the station you are born to fill'[10]. He couldn't have been more wrong. 'The very comfortable little wife,'[11] was to be anything but.

From the off, George and Caroline hated each other. She arrived in England expecting to see the pretty young man from his official portraits, but George had started to fill out. As Caroline bemoaned his fading good looks, George called for brandy to chase away the stink of his newly arrived betrothed. But despite their mutual complaints, there could be no going back. The king and the people of Britain alike were tired of George's profligacy and scandal, so they welcomed Caroline with open arms. The plans were laid for a glittering ceremony that would take place on 8 April 1795.

> 'At about a quarter before nine the Princess entered the Chapel [at St James's Palace]. The Overture of Esther was performed while the procession was entering. As soon as the ROYAL FAMILY had taken their seats, and all the personages in the procession had reached the places assigned them, the ceremony began; It was performed by his

Grace the Archbishop of CANTERBURY, with the most dignified
solemnity.

Her Royal Highness the PRINCESS [Caroline] seemed a little
fluttered upon her first entering the Chapel, but perfectly regained
her composure before the commencement of the Ceremony – Her
manner was easy, affable and engaging in the highest degree. – The
PRINCE displayed the most amiable sensibility, and seemed so
much affected at one time as to be unable to repeat the necessary
part of the Ceremony after the Archbishop. The whole scene was
awful, affecting and sublime.'[12]

But this report doesn't tell anything like the full story. The groom wasn't
affected by the overwhelming emotion of the occasion at all. In fact, the
groom was drunk. George was so paralytic that he couldn't even stand
and in between sobbing, slurring and staggering, he had to be held
upright by groomsmen who struggled to keep him on his feet.

Later, when things had fatally fallen apart, Caroline related what came
next to Lady Charlotte Campbell Bury. It wasn't exactly a happy wedding
night.

'What it was to have a drunken husband on one's wedding-day, and
one who passed the greatest part of his bridal-night under the grate,
where fell, and where I left him. If anybody say to me at dis [sic]
moment – will you pass your life over again, or be killed? I would
choose death; for you know, a little sooner or later we must all die;
but to live a life of wretchedness twice over, - oh! mine God, no!'[13]

And things got progressively worse. George was hardly a gentleman
when it came to his wife. He accused her of lacking even basic personal
hygiene and worse still, told anyone who cared to listen that Caroline
wasn't a virgin on her wedding night. Now, let's not forget that the prince
was *far* from untouched when he collapsed into the hearth after their
wedding, but for him that didn't matter. What mattered was that 'on the
first night was there no appearance of blood, but her manners were not
those of a novice.'[14] He claimed to have physical evidence too and went
on to claim that 'finding that I had suspicions of her not being new, she
the next night mixed up some tooth powder and water [and] coloured her

shift with it [...] I made a vow never to touch her again. I had known her three times - twice the first and once the second night.'[15]

What a charmer. Yet clearly something had happened in between the fighting, because the two of them weren't to stay a twosome for long.

'The Princess of WALES and the little Infant both promise to do well. The enquiries after them at Carlton House were yesterday so numerous, that Pall-mall was quite thronged with carriages.'[16]

Despite George only 'knowing' Caroline three times, it was enough to result in a pregnancy. Almost nine months to the day from that unfortunate wedding night, the Prince and Princess of Wales welcomed their only child to the world. Sadly, the new-born Princess Charlotte was born into a marriage that had already become a war of attrition.

The Split

'We have, unfortunately, been oblig'd to acknowledge to each other that we cannot find happiness in our Union. Circumstances of character & education which it is needless to discuss now, render that impossible. It then only remains that we should make the situation as little uncomfortable to each other, as its nature will allow. It has been my studious wish to soften it in that respect to You. [...] Let me therefore beg of You to make the best of a situation unfortunate for us both, which is only to be done by not *wantonly creating*, or magnifying, uncomfortable circumstances.'[17]

When the Prince of Wales wrote to his wife in April 1796 to tell her that they should try and part without animosity, their marriage was already effectively over. Though the king continued to be supportive of Caroline and blamed his son's shameless gadding about for the split, there was likely no preventing it. Caroline left for a new life at Blackheath, where she was to become one of her estranged husband's greatest enemies. There she presided over her own court where the prince's opponents were made shamelessly welcome. In Carlton House, George fumed over rumours of his wife's amorous adventures with his political opponents and to make matters worse, the public lapped it up. It seemed that nothing could stop the Princess of Wales from being the darling of the British public.

George was desperate to unmask Caroline as an immoral gadabout and in 1802 he was sure he had found the smoking gun. An infant named William Austin appeared in the house at Blackheath and Caroline's former friend, Lady Douglas, told the prince that this was no charity child. Instead, she claimed, *little Willikins* was the bastard son of the Princess of Wales, sired by an unknown lover.

The prince swung into action and demanded that Caroline be held to account for her potentially treasonous actions. After all, what better proof of an adulterous tryst than the presence of a child? To put an end to the matter a supposedly secret enquiry named the Delicate Investigation was called under the watchful eye of the prime minister, William Grenville. It was entrusted with determining whether Caroline had committed adultery and if so, whether the little boy was the product of that liaison. Should she be found guilty, then the gentlemen on the committee of the Delicate Investigation would be required to determine the appropriate punishment. Caroline could be sure of one thing: it would be harsh indeed.

In fact, Caroline didn't give a fig for the Delicate Investigation because she had a trump card waiting up her sleeve. As the learned gentlemen debated the behaviour of the Princess of Wales and the parentage of William Austin, Caroline's advisor, future prime minister Spencer Perceval, produced the witnesses who would stop the investigation in its tracks. They were a poor couple named Sophia and Samuel Austin and far from being the illegitimate fruit of a treasonous liaison, William was their little boy. The benevolent princess had taken him into her household when his parents could no longer afford his care. She wasn't a sinner; she was a saint. Surprisingly, in an age before forensic tests, this was all the proof Caroline needed to prove her innocence.

'[The] generous people of England will feel that this illustrious and amiable PRINCESS has a stronger title than ever to their attached and affectionate support,'[18] trumpeted the *Morning Post*. For the Prince of Wales, things could hardly get worse.

Though the parentage of William was settled, the enquiry stopped short of completely exonerating Caroline of adultery. George scored a bitter victory of sorts when Caroline's access to her daughter, Charlotte, was restricted in the aftermath of the investigation. It wasn't much, but it was still something.

The Regent

'That a loyal and dutiful address be presented to his Royal Highness the Prince Regent, condoling with him on the melancholy affliction of our most gracious Sovereign, which have rendered him incapable of the personal exercise of the royal functions; lamenting the unnecessary restrictions which have been placed on his Royal Highness, in supplying the deficiency of the executive power; expressing a perfect confidence in the known virtues and endowments of his Royal Highness; and relying that, in the present difficult and embarrassing situation of affairs, every measure, which depends *personally* on his Royal Highness, for promoting the peace, happiness, and welfare of the country, would be adopted.'[19]

King George III was not well. His mental health had been in turmoil for years but the death of his youngest surviving child, Amelia, proved to be the killer blow for his wits. The king's eyesight had failed as his body slowly gave up and though he struggled to get around, he'd still made a daily visit to sit beside the bed of Amelia, who was suffering with consumption. The 27-year-old princess and her father had always shared a quiet, mutually adoring relationship and when she died on 2 November 1810, it shattered the monarch. For a man who was already struggling with his sovereign duties, there was no question that the death of Amelia was anything but catastrophic.

In Parliament those loyal Whigs who had waited patiently for the Prince of Wales to take his place on the throne now held their breath. With the king so obviously indisposed the only alternative was to propose a Regency and once again, the clear candidate for the job was George. After spending much of the last twenty-five years in opposition, the Whigs prepared for a triumphant return to government once the Prince of Wales reigned as Regent. The fact that he had taken the oaths of office standing beside a bust of his late friend, Charles James Fox, was seen as an omen of blessings to come.

In fact, the Whigs were about to get a surprise. Though the Prince of Wales did indeed become Regent when *The Care of King During his Illness, etc. Act 1811* was passed, he didn't immediately overturn the Tory status quo at all. Instead, when he assumed power on 5 February 1811, the new Regent's first act was to throw the sort of party that he had always loved. It was showy, loud and expensive and his new subjects were appalled. In their eyes, it showcased everything that was bad about the flighty prince. What they wanted was a solemn and dignified handing over of power, in which the king's eldest son acknowledged his new role without pomp and with due respect to his father. What they got was a knees-up.

Once the celebrations were over, the Whigs, including the Regent's daughter, Charlotte, waited for the brand-new Prince Regent to call them to power. Instead they found themselves disappointed. Far from dismissing the Tories and summoning the Whigs, Prinny decided to leave things exactly as they were. Central to his decision was the belief that his father, already in dire straits, wouldn't cope well with such a wholesale and tumultuous change. Prinny may have behaved badly at times, but even *he* knew when to stop.

Don't be fooled into believing that the Regent had finally discovered a hidden streak of sensitivity though, as Maria Fitzherbert was to discover. It was in 1811 that the far from fairy tale romance of the prince and the widow ended forever. Though it had been on and off a few times, it was an invitation to dinner that finally sealed her fate.

By the time he became Regent, George had long since moved on from Lady Jersey to his latest amour, Isabella Ingram-Seymour-Conway, Marchioness of Hertford. She was on the guest list for a glittering dinner at Carlton House in 1811 and so was Maria Fitzherbert. Yet when the invitations went out, Maria was informed that she would be seated at the far end of the table, as far from the Prince Regent as possible. When Maria was advised that this was in keeping with her lowly rank, she wasn't impressed. Maria cut her last ties with her secret husband there and then. She declined the invitation and the two never met again. Indeed, they never communicated at all until George was on his deathbed and Maria sent him one final letter of goodbye.

But the Prince Regent wasn't yet done with trouble from the ladies in his life.

To Wed a Daughter

While all of this was going on, George's relationships with his daughter and estranged wife were going from bad to worse. When Charlotte was very young, she had been packed off to live in Montague House whilst her father gadded about with his mistresses. With her mother's access to her restricted, Caroline and Charlotte were forced into secret meetings thanks to sympathetic ladies in the little princess' household. As Charlotte grew up, she displayed more than a little of her parents' love of the spotlight, blowing kisses to senior Whigs from her box at the opera and even on one occasion running away from home and jumping into a cab to escape to her mother's house. She only returned when her Whig friends convinced her that things would be all the worse for Caroline if she didn't.

George knew all about the agony of being forced into an unwanted marriage, but that didn't stop him from resolving to subject his daughter to such a fate. She was the heir to the throne, and it was vital that she make a good match or, more to the point, that her father make a good match for her. After some consideration, Prinny decided that there could be no better candidate than William, Prince of Orange. Charlotte was horrified at the thought of such a union, but for the Prince Regent, what Charlotte wanted was unimportant.

When she learned of the intended marriage between Charlotte and Orange, Queen Charlotte, the prospective bride's grandmother, took up her pen and wrote to her son. Though far from effusive, her missive no doubt reflects his own feelings on the matter.

> 'My dearest Son.
>
> Your Kindness of charging the Duke of York with the Commission of acquainting me with the intended Alliance between Your Daughter & the Hereditary Prince of Orange calls for my most gratefull [sic] acknowledgement. My Congratulations upon this Event. You will not doubt to be Sincere when I say, may this Union prove to be as Happy as Your own hath been Fatal.'[20]

In fact, the union didn't happen at all. Princess Charlotte's flight from home had been a last-ditch protest intended to force her father to listen to her complaints about the planned nuptials, and it did just that. George's own arranged marriage had been miserable and Charlotte, who had grown up witnessing the war of attrition, had no doubt that hers would be too. As pig-headed as ever, Prinny had already signed the marriage contracts and was planning to ship Charlotte out of London and into the seclusion of Cranbourne Lodge at Windsor, but her escape drove a coach and horses through those plans. The young princess was a public favourite and so was her mother, who added her voice to support Charlotte's pleas to be released from the marriage contract. There was another man she wanted, Charlotte admitted, and his name was Prince Leopold of Saxe-Coburg-Saalfeld.

Charlotte got her way. George called off the engagement and agreed to an audience with Prince Leopold. Though the Regent made no promises, Princess Charlotte was convinced that her beloved would charm her father into saying *yes* to their hoped-for marriage. Caroline of Brunswick was all for it, but what assistance she could offer was limited since she had left Great Britain for a new life on the continent. What Charlotte *did* have was public support. When the Princess of Wales and her daughter wanted something, they usually spoke for Britain too.

In fact, the young princess had nothing to fear because when her father met Prince Leopold, he was as bowled over as Charlotte was. The wedding was arranged without delay and on 2 May 1816, the happy couple were joined at Carlton House.

'Two crimson velvet stools were placed in front of the altar, which was covered with crimson velvet. There was some ancient royal communion-plate on the altar, with two superb candlesticks six feet high.

[...]

Her Royal Highness the Princess Charlotte advanced to the altar with much steadiness, and went through the ceremony, giving the responses with great clearness, so as to be heard distinctly by every person present. Prince Leopold was not heard so distinctly. The Regent gave away the bride.

As soon as the ceremony was concluded, the Princess Charlotte embraced her father, and went up to the Queen, whose hand she kissed with respectful affection. Each of the Princesses her Royal Highness kissed, and then shook hands with her illustrious uncles. The bride and bridegroom retired arm in arm, and soon after set off for Oatlands, which they reached at ten minutes before twelve.'[21]

The marriage of Charlotte and Leopold was that rare thing amongst dynastic unions, a happy one. Sadly, it would be short-lived and ended in a tragedy that shook the nation.

'It is this day our melancholy duty to make known to our Readers, the demise of her Royal Highness the Princess CHARLOTTE. This young, beautiful, and interesting Princess survived the delivery of a still born child but a few hours. The shock which this unexpected and afflicting event gave yesterday morning to the loyal and affectionate inhabitants of the Metropolis, cannot be adequately described, and it will be equally felt throughout every part of his Majesty's dominions.'[22]

The Prince Regent's only child died after delivering a stillborn son. It plunged the country into mourning and the House of Hanover into a whirlpool of broken hearts and hasty marriages, as we will learn later.

The Errant Wife

When Princess Charlotte died, her mother was living life to the full on the continent. Free from the husband she'd hated, Caroline's life had become one of parties, travel and fun, all undertaken in the company of her *chamberlain*, Bartolomeo Pergami. Pergami had met the princess in Italy when he called at her hotel hoping to secure employment. He found a lady with her gown caught in the furniture and after he had released her from her predicament, she introduced herself as the Princess of Wales. From that moment, the couple was inseparable, but Pergami's presence in Caroline's life was a fresh thorn in George's side. How dare she be happy, he raged, when he was anything but the darling of the people.

George and Caroline had been estranged for two decades but when Charlotte passed away, their mutual animosity flared into war. The Prince Regent didn't bother to let Caroline know that her only daughter had died. She found out quite by accident, when she unexpectedly encountered a royal messenger who was passing through the Italian village where she was residing on his way to deliver word of the death to the pope. When Caroline asked whose death he was charged with reporting, she learned that it was that of her only child. From that moment on, her fury knew no bounds.

What Caroline didn't know was that her husband had another card to play. George wanted a divorce more than anything and he was determined to get it. He dispatched agents to Europe to infiltrate Caroline's household and collect evidence for the so-called Milan Commission to prove that she was guilty of adultery. When he had the evidence, he was determined to press for the divorce he longed for, whatever the cost.

But things weren't going to be quite so easy as all that.

As the Regent's spies were assembling their evidence in Italy, Queen Charlotte died. Her eldest son was at her side. She was one of the only people who could control his more outrageous behaviour and without her, George was bereft. He was also more unpopular than ever thanks to his uncompromisingly luxurious lifestyle, as his subjects suffered deprivations caused by the cost of Britain's war effort on the continent. Vandals daubed 'Bread, or the Regent's Head' on the walls of Carlton House and when Prinny rode out in his carriage, stones were hurled as he passed. He had no head for public relations and had singularly failed to capitalize on the wave of goodwill that followed Wellington's victory at Waterloo, so it seems only fitting that Peterloo would put the last nail in the coffin of his popularity.

On 16 August 1819 a peaceful rally was held at St Peter's Field, Manchester, by the Manchester Patriotic Union Society. In a land where people were starving and suffrage was denied to the working classes, tens of thousands of citizens gathered to listen to speakers call for equality. Many children were included in the peaceful audience of 60,000. Faced with the size of the crowd, magistrate William Hulton gave an order to arrest the speakers and disperse the meeting. His requests for armed intervention were met with marked enthusiasm by the men of the Manchester and Salford Yeomanry, whose mounted Hussars charged the crowd with sabres drawn. When the smoke cleared, the ground was littered with the dead and wounded. Journalists sympathetic to the cause of the rally were taken into custody and those who had spoken on the day were committed for trial on charges of high treason.

As the public protested against the injustice and demanded that the Hussars be arrested and tried, the Prince Regent took the opposite stance. He spoke out in support of the military intervention, plunging his public standing to a new low. Whilst his ailing father was lauded and eulogised by his subjects as he lived in seclusion at Windsor, the Prince Regent was hated. But if he thought things couldn't get any worse, he was to be badly mistaken. In fact, the death of George III ushered his son into a whole new world of trouble.

> 'The last sad moments of the life of our Gracious Sovereign were undisturbed by pain. – Nature seemed to have been exhausted, and he died, as we have stated, at thirty-five minutes past eight, without indicating any appearance of bodily suffering.'[23]

The Prince Regent was a Regent no longer. He was a king at last.

Pains and Penalties

George was finally on the throne as king and that meant the distinct possibility that his estranged wife might expect to be named queen at his forthcoming coronation. So desperate was George to avoid this that he was prepared to put everything very publicly on the line in pursuit of his longed-for divorce. From the start, the public mood was ugly and very definitely in favour of Caroline. The people of Great Britain were horrified that George had employed Caroline's own servants to gather evidence against her, especially when he openly and shamelessly flaunted his own paramours. For her part, Caroline wasn't going to go quietly. She believed that she had every right to be called queen and, still smarting from the painful snub over Charlotte's death, was determined to make her point and cause her husband as much anguish and embarrassment as was possible. She planned to kill with kindness.

'[Lord Brougham] had to express on her Majesty's behalf, the satisfaction she felt that there was an end of all secret, unconstitutional, and illegal inquiry, and that she was at length to have a public trial.'[24]

Aware of the difficulties that would be presented should Caroline attempt to attend the coronation, Parliament did its best to keep her away and even offered a generously increased allowance should she agree to remain on the continent, but Caroline was having none of it. Instead she came back to England, to be greeted at Dover by a rapturous public. From the port to the city the streets were lined with people ready to celebrate her return, calling, 'Long live Queen Caroline!', much to George's chagrin.

'As her Majesty's carriage decended [sic] the hill towards London [...] It may be doubted whether, since the days of Queen Elizabeth, when Greenwich was a royal seat, and when festivals and aquatic spectacles first laid the basis of its importance, its neighbourhood has ever presented a more lively scene.'[25]

Caroline was ready to meet George head on and with the Pains and Penalties Bill waiting, she would need all her fighting spirit. The Bill would put Caroline on trial in the House of Lords to determine if she had committed adultery. If she was found guilty, the divorce would be agreed, and Caroline would be stripped of all her British titles and rank. Not only that, but her reputation would be utterly decimated.

'The question before the tribunal is – whether a Lady, claiming the rights, dignities, sanctities, honours, patronages and pre-eminencies of a Queen Consort of the glorious Crown of England has not publicly lived in criminal cohabitation with *Mr. Bergami* [sic], whatever *Bergami* may have been, *Courier* or *Count. That* is the question – *and* NO OTHER.'[26]

To the people of a country that was already at boiling point, it wasn't just the queen who was on trial, but liberty itself. As the prosecution called forth the witnesses who had spied on Caroline during her continental gadabout, the mood of the nation grew darker and dislike of the king grew more fervent than ever. The public had adored George III and Queen Charlotte for their mutual and faithful devotion in spite of some tumultuous years but in George IV they saw nothing but profligacy and bad behaviour. In a world where poverty was rife and suffering was an everyday occurrence, the new king lived high on the hog with seemingly no thought for what his subjects were going through. They were damned if they were going to support him now.

Caroline retained as her counsel Lord Brougham, one of the keenest legal minds of the era. He didn't particularly care for his client, nor did he believe that she was pure innocence so much as, according to Brougham, 'pure in no sense', but he relished the drama of the trial. He cut a swathe through the witnesses for the prosecution, getting the upper hand at every turn. Caroline was so unconcerned by the outcome that she played card games in an ante room or even dozed off during the proceedings whilst in Carlton House, her would-be tormentor watched as his plans began to fall apart. George pinned all his hopes on Theodore Majocchi, once one of Caroline's most trusted staff, now the star witness for the prosecution. When Majocchi appeared in the dock Caroline was ruffled for the first time and with an exclamation of his name, she fled the Chamber. If George took that to be a sign of impending victory, he was mistaken.

Brougham didn't just shake Majocchi, he destroyed him. When he answered questions for the prosecution, the former servant could remember even the tiniest scandalous details and painted a picture of a debauched household in which Caroline and Pergami shared beds, baths and even a chamber pot. When Brougham questioned him, however, his previously infallible memory deserted him. To every question Majocchi answered, '*non mi ricordo*', which translates as 'I don't remember.' Soon he found he had unwittingly acquired a catchphrase. People jeered him in the London streets, bellowing *non mi ricordo* after him as he passed.

The Pains and Penalties Bill was a public relations disaster. Once it passed the Lords by just nine votes, it went no further. Lord Liverpool, the prime minister and a keen opponent of Caroline of Brunswick, gauged the public mood and knew that there was no sense in presenting the Bill to the Commons where it would face almost certain defeat. At first George refused to take his advice and pull the Bill, but Liverpool prevailed. Caroline was victorious. There was to be no divorce.

The End of Caroline

By the time his coronation came around in July 1821, George IV was no longer the glamorous, pretty fashionista he had once been. Instead he was on the cusp of 60, his weight ever-increasing and his health failing, but he still knew how to party. Caroline might have won the popular victory but as far as her husband was concerned, she wasn't on the guest list for his Westminster Abbey coronation, nor was she welcome at the nationwide booze up that was to follow. Caroline, of course, had other ideas.

It wasn't simply because she wanted to share the spotlight – though she did, even if her supporters claimed that, 'Her Majesty, while she despised the idle pomp and ceremony of the coronation, was well aware that important right and prerogatives were connected with it,'[27] – but because she honestly believed that she had a right to be there as the wife of the king. As the date of the coronation approached, Caroline wrote to her husband asking for details of the big day. She wanted to know what he would like her to wear, if there was anything in particular she needed to do and whether there was any other pertinent information, given that she would be crowned alongside him as his wife. For George, this was beyond the pale. He asked Lord Liverpool to let Caroline know that she wasn't welcome. Even her advisor, Brougham, told her that her attendance at the coronation would be an affront to decency, but her mind was made up.

On the big day Caroline arrived at Westminster Abbey at 6.00 am, accompanied by the gentlemanly Lord Hood. As the gathered crowds watched, the two made their way from door to door, asking to be admitted. At every turn they received the same humiliating reply: Lord Hood, safely in possession of an invitation, was welcome. Caroline was not. The chivalrous gentleman offered the queen his own invitation, but she rejected it, determined that she would attend not as a guest, but as the wife of the monarch. All of this was marvellous entertainment to the bored crowd that had arrived at dawn but unlike her past escapades, this one wasn't winning Caroline any friends. The people who had assembled at Westminster Abbey at daybreak weren't there for drama, they were there for a party. Once the Pains and Penalties Bill was finished the public had expected Caroline to return triumphant to the continent, but she had hung around instead. She'd committed the cardinal sin of celebrity – she'd missed her moment to leave them wanting more. It was an embarrassment from which she never recovered. Within the month, Caroline of Brunswick was dead.

As the doorkeepers turned Caroline away, the crowd jeered her. She fled back to her carriage and left the king to enjoy one of the most glittering and expensive coronations the world had ever witnessed. The festivities cost more than £200,000 and lasted for hours, with a grand Jacobean-themed procession into the Abbey followed by the lengthy and red hot ceremony, throughout which the king laboured and perspired in a black hat adorned with ostrich and heron plumes, as well as £24,000 worth of robes, including a crimson velvet train which measured a breath taking 27 feet in length and was tended by eight pages. George completed the look with a brand-new crown containing 12,000 rented diamonds from Rundell, Bridge and Rundell[28]. The king was showing off his very best bling.

After hours in the stifling confines of Westminster Abbey, the big moment came. As the crown was placed on George's head, the ancient walls rang to the huzzahs of the probably rather relieved congregation. The corpulent king headed from the sweltering abbey to Westminster Hall and the feast to end all feasts, which went on deep into the night. Across the country, parties were thrown, and fireworks ignited, all in celebration of the once loathed sovereign. When there was a party to attend, all was forgiven.

And what of Caroline?

The story of the uncrowned queen ended with her death from an intestinal obstruction on 7 August 1821. On the matter of his widowhood, the king had little to say, but he wrote to his private secretary, Sir William Knighton, and admitted that the unexpected good news, 'which the fortuitous Hand of God, in His mercy, has bestowed upon me, in this recent event, is so great [that] it affords me a fair prospect of real & true happiness for the rest of my Days.'[29]

But those days were disappearing fast.

The King is Dead

As the years passed, the widowed king had no interest in marrying again. He was perfectly content in the company of his mistress, Elizabeth, Marchioness Conyngham, and she revelled in her high-status affair. Though George had still been entangled with Isabella Ingram–Seymour–Conway, Marchioness of Hertford, when he met Lady Conyngham in 1819, by 1820, Lady C was his one and only. The Duke of Wellington claimed that Lady Conyngham had nursed an ambition to be the king's mistress for years and would have stopped at nothing to achieve her goal. By the time of the coronation, there was no doubt that Lady Conyngham had reached the top.

The diarist Harriet Arbuthnot recalled the ceremony at Westminster Abbey and wrote that:

> 'The King behaved very indecently; he was continually nodding & winking at Ly Conyngham & sighing & making eyes at her. At one time in the Abbey he took a diamond brooch from his breast &, looking at her, kissed it, on which she took off her glove & kissed a ring she had on!! Anybody who could have seen his disgusting figure, with a wig the curls of which hung down his back, & quite bending beneath the weight of his robes & his 60 years would have been quite sick.'[30]

Lady Conyngham was a permanent fixture until the end of her lover's life. He allowed her to wear the Stuart Sapphire, one of the Crown Jewels, and when she wasn't measuring out his laudanum dosage, she was busy feathering her own nest. As Dorothea Lieven, the wife of the Russian ambassador, memorably reflected, Lady Conyngham had 'not a word to say for herself, nothing but a hand to accept pearls and diamonds with, and an enormous balcony to wear them on.'[31] That remarkable *balcony* was never far from the king in the final decade of his life, propping him up as his health grew ever more frail.

With his weight ballooning and his reliance on laudanum and alcohol greater than ever, George retired to Windsor just as George III had in the final decades of his own life. Yet George IV's health problems were physical rather than mental, exacerbated by his immense size and addictions. He was so paranoid about his weight that he eventually withdrew from society, spending more and more time alone or in the company of a select group that included Lady Conyngham and his beloved young niece, Victoria.

In 1830, George was virtually immobile and was blighted by failing sight. When Maria Fitzherbert heard of her husband's predicament, she sent him one final letter to say goodbye, but he was too ill to pick up his pen and reply. George's horizons had shrunk down from a vast kingdom to a single room, where he slept in a bespoke chair that could be converted into a bed. He suffered from constant agonies that no amount of bloodletting or laudanum could soothe, even when administered by Sir Henry Halford, the famed royal physician.

George IV's suffering came to an end on 26 June 1830 just before 3.15 am. He was 67. Attended by his friend and physician, Sir Jonathan Wathen Waller, the ailing king passed a near-sleepless night. Quite out of nowhere, he reached out and grasped at Wathen Waller's hand, gasping, 'My boy, this is death'.

And he was right.

> 'His Majesty had been becoming weaker for some days past. At ten o'clock last night the King appeared sleepy; and, in consequence, Sir Henry Halford, Sir Matthew Tierney, and Mr Brodie, left his Majesty, leaving Sir Wathen Waller, and also two of the pages in attendance. The King slept at intervals till three o'clock, when his Majesty awoke and expressed a wish to be raised up. While preparing to raise the King it was discovered that his Majesty was in so alarming a state that Sir Wathen Waller had Sir Henry Halford, Sir Matthew Tierney, Sir W. Knighton, and Mr Brodie called up. All these gentlemen came into the apartment in a few minutes, and they had not been in there five minutes before his Majesty expired.'[32]

As George was laid to rest with Maria Fitzherbert's miniature around his neck, *The Times* venomously commented, 'If [the king] ever had a friend – a devoted friend in any rank of life – we protest that the name of him or her never reached us'[33]. The legend of the leviathan of the Haut Ton has only grown in death. It's fair to say that the country never saw his like again, for better or worse.

Act Three

Frederick, Duke of York and Albany
(16 August 1763–5 January 1827)

The Favourite Son

'AUSPICIOUS *August* does this isle adorn;
To us another British Prince is *born*;
The Fates, Britannia, with your wish combine,
Behold another pledge in Brunswick's line;
A pledge to Briton to secure our cause,
Our rights, religion, liberties and laws.
When Wallis's Prince's birth did bless our isle,
The clouds dropp'd fatness and made Britain smile.
See now auspicious *too*, the second birth,
Sol's rays mature the produce of the earth.
In grateful thanks to heaven, then Britons sing,
Both babes a blessing did so Briton bring.'[1]

When it came to the upbringing of the eldest sons of George III and Queen Charlotte, there was little to differentiate one from the next. As the little boys grew up in the stifling atmosphere of the royal household, Frederick soon became his father's favourite of the older sons, but he was still expected to behave as a prince should.

When Frederick was just six months old, he was elected to the position of Prince-Bishop of Osnabrück, a hereditary role that had been in the partial gift of the family from Hanover for generations. Its fate had been decided more than a century before Frederick's birth by the Treaty of Westphalia, which brought the Thirty Years' War to an end. Amongst its many complicated rulings was the decision that the bishopric would henceforth alternate between Catholic and Protestant rule. In the case of the latter, the religious duties of the postholder were delegated to the bishopric's clerics, so in real terms, having the titleholder as a babe-in-arms had little impact on day to day life in Osnabrück, though it brought with it a handsome annual income for the young prince. It was agreed that Frederick could be appointed to the Prince-Bishopric on the understanding that he would spend a prolonged period of his youth in Germany, so that he might reasonably claim to be familiar with the country's customs and concerns. His father dutifully agreed.

Though Germany would eventually beckon, in his formative years, Frederick remained in England where he was subject to the same ceaseless lessons and strict discipline as his brother. Like the Prince of Wales, Frederick was expected to be as pious and dedicated to duty as his parents. In fact, he would prove to share many of his elder brother's vices but unlike the heir to the throne, he was also possessed of a sense of responsibility that might not have been as tireless as that of George III, but was still far in excess of anything the Prince of Wales ever exhibited. Frederick, let us not forget, was the *spare* to George's *heir* but should no unforeseen tragedy occur, his life would take a very different path to that of his brother. Whilst George longed for a military career that he simply couldn't have, no such obstacles stood in Frederick's path.

Frederick loved the outdoor life and from an early age he had his heart set on a military career. It was this that endeared him to his father, who saw in his second son the duty and dedication that his eldest seemed to lack. Frederick even did his best to advise his brother on how to maintain good relations with the king, who he understood instinctively. 'Consider he is vexed enough in publick [sic] affairs,' he wrote, 'it is therefore your business not to make that still worse.'[2] George wouldn't listen, of course, and Frederick wouldn't always be there to provide him with counsel when it came to family relations.

Just as George had developed his love for women early, Frederick also had a weakness for ladies, although he was rather plain and did not share his brother's good looks. By the age of 17 he was already entangled with Letitia Smith[3], the mistress of highwayman John Rann, but Frederick's relationship with Ms Smith wasn't to last. How could it, when the prince was destined for the soldiers' life?

Germany

By the time he turned 17, Frederick was ready to fly the nest. He longed to go to America and join the fighting there but first he had to honour the commitment his father had made, and he was forced to spend a prolonged period in Germany. Frederick was given the rank of colonel in the British army at the start of November 1780 and just weeks later said his emotional farewells to his family. Then he set out to begin his new life in Germany.

Frederick was greeted by a welcoming crowd and settled quickly, even as the Prince of Wales mourned the loss of his best friend back home in England. Frederick enrolled at the University of Göttingen, learned to speak German and threw himself into military studies where he was kept busy reviewing troops and getting used to the practicalities of army life. The king received glowing reports of Frederick's endeavours, and within a year of his arrival in Germany, George had his son promoted to the rank of major-general. He was a marvellous ambassador for the British crown and during a tour of Germany even impressed Frederick the Great, who invited him to inspect the Prussian troops, then showered the young prince with glittering receptions in his honour.

As the two Fredericks strutted their stuff on the continent, at home, George III was battling with his eldest son, whose scandalous behaviour and love of the high life was rarely out of the papers. The king took some comfort in the fact that he could at least credit himself with the good behaviour of Frederick. When Frederick's wilful younger brothers, William and Edward, joined him in Germany, the king naturally hoped that some of his elder son's influence might rub off on them and waited eagerly for Frederick's regular progress reports on his siblings. Sadly, as we will learn later, the news wasn't always good.

As they watched their *spare* flourish, George and Charlotte could slap themselves on the back for a job well done. It was a sign of the king's admiration for Frederick that George III created him Duke of York and Albany in November 1784 and bestowed upon him a yearly income of £12,000, much to his son's delight.

'I have this moment received your Majesty's letter of the 30th of November in which you are so good as to communicate to me your having been graciously pleased to create me Duke of York and

Albany. […] It would require much more time was I to endeavour to express the whole of my feelings upon these repeated marks of your Majesty's favour and kindness towards me.'[4]

The king's trust was demonstrated in a more concrete manner when Frederick was appointed as one of the Lords of the Regency of Hanover, which gave him executive powers over the ancestral electorate. In this new role he could steer Hanover through the establishment of the *Fürstenbund*, or *League of Princes*, which protected the existing German states against any threat from the ambitious Emperor Joseph II, ruler of the Holy Roman Empire.

It seemed that wherever Frederick went in Germany, he met with success. Both he and the king prayed that his dedication would rub off on the younger princes and one detects the hand of George III in a cautionary letter that Frederick wrote to his brother, William. William had long been a cause for parental concern thanks to his apparent proclivity for the life of an able seaman rather than that of an officer, and Frederick hoped that a little reminder of how even princes could end up rudderless might pull him back into line.

> 'Let me, My Dearest William Give You the advice of now applying yourself strenuously to Your Profession, Consider that as both of us must rise faster in our different Lines than others, We have less time left us to learn, for only think a moment of the Situation of our two Uncles the Dukes of Gloucester and Cumberland who at this alarming moment, are at home unemployed because it is impossible to give them any Commands as they are so totally ignorant of the Professions into which they have entered.'[5]

As we will see later, William didn't exactly heed the warning of his wiser older brother when it came to his studies. Despite several of the princes spending prolonged periods in Germany, it was Frederick who the king really trusted in his familial electorate. He could rely on Fredrick's keen military mind to accurately report on the machinations of the Holy Roman Emperor as well as other leaders in the region, and when Frederick the Great invited the prince to attend his celebrated review of the entire Prussian army, there was no doubting that the young Duke of York and Albany made a great impression on the famed monarch.

Compared with the Prince of Wales' womanising and spending, it might seem that the Duke of York's conduct was simply too good to be true. In fact, he had plenty of vices of his own. Just like George, he enjoyed the lure of the gaming table, where he was introduced to Baron Seltenheim, a scandalous German nobleman and thoroughly bad influence. It wasn't only gambling that took Frederick's fancy and when he met Princess Frederica Charlotte of Prussia, the great-niece of Frederick the Great, he was smitten. Though she would later become his bride, there was still one thing that was more tempting than romance. What Frederick longed for more than anything was to go home.

While the Prince of Wales was begging for money from the king and government to pay his debts, Frederick's income from the Osnabrück bishopric had been safely kept in trust by the king. He now instructed his father that he wished to purchase Lord Galway's estate near Knaresborough and return to England to live there. At first George resisted, explaining apologetically that he was currently engaged in an argument over finances with the Prince of Wales. Should Frederick come home and throw his support behind the king, this would inevitably lead to a fracture between the two brothers. Having been estranged from his own siblings, the monarch wished to avoid this at all costs. Though Frederick wasn't happy with the response, he honoured his father's wishes and stayed in Germany. From the following passage, it's clear to see how maturely Frederick conducted himself and why the king had placed such trust in his sober-minded son.

'[If George III] should still persevere in thinking that the present moment is an unfavourable one, I can only say that I shall with infinite regret give up the idea that I have entertained of paying my respects to your Majesty and the Queen in the course of this Winter, and I am sure your Majesty is too just not to excuse the eagerness with which I have endeavoured to combat every objection which can be produced towards deferring my return after an absence of very near six years from those whom I have every reason to love and respect.'[6]

On this occasion, Frederick was to remain disappointed, but his disappointment was relatively short-lived. In February 1787, the sovereign declared that the time had come and summoned Frederick to Britain. Though the journey would be a long one and he wouldn't set foot on British soil until the summer, the Duke of York and Albany could finally come home.

The Regency Crisis

The Prince of Wales, who had longed to become a soldier, would never see active service. Instead he was confined to a ceremonial role, dressing up in his collection of magnificent uniforms to review the troops who he would never join in battle. The Duke of York, meanwhile, was living his brother's dream, gadding around Germany watching manoeuvres with a rank that meant something. George III had prevented his second son from coming home sooner for fear that he might argue with the Prince of Wales over money but when the moment to choose allegiances came, the king was proved wrong. When Frederick was forced to take sides with his brother or his parents, he chose the Prince of Wales.

When he arrived in England Frederick headed to Allerton Mauleverer, his new country residence in North Yorkshire, but he soon found that it was too far from London to suit his needs. He sold the estate – though some gossips believed he had lost it in a card game – and took up residence at Oatlands Park in Surrey instead. Settled once more, he resumed his friendship with the Prince of Wales and was soon a member of his glittering and fashionable social circle. If Frederick's letters to the king had been those of a sober and serious young man, a few months in London and membership of Brooks's, the fashionable and wealthy club where the Prince of Wales was a leading light, was all it took to bring out the wayward side of the Duke of York.

> 'The Duke of York, Colonel St. Leger, Tom Stepney, and two others, one morning, about three o'clock, came reeling along Pall Mall, highly charged with the juice of the grape and ripe for a row. Meeting with nothing worthy of their attention, they entered St. James's-street and soon arrived at Brookes's, where they kicked and knocked most loudly for admission.
>
> [...]

No sooner said than done: when they arrived in the inner hall, they commenced the destruction of chairs, tables, and chandeliers, and kicked up such a horrible din as might have awakened the dead.

[...]

During this *mêlée* there was no light; and the uproar made by the maid-servants, who, in the confusion, rushed into the arms of our heroes, and expected nothing short of immediate violence and murder, was most tremendous.

At length, one of the waiters ran for a loaded blunderbuss, which having cocked, and rested on an angle of the banisters, he would have discharged amongst the intruders. From doing this, however, he was most providentially deterred by the housekeeper, who, with no other covering than her chemise and flannel-petticoat, was fast approaching with a light, which no sooner flashed upon the faces of these midnight disturbers, than she exclaimed, "For Heaven's sake, Tom, don't fire! it is only the Duke of York!"-- The terror of the servants having vanished by this timely address, the intruding party soon became more peaceable, and were sent home in sedan-chairs to their respective places of residence.'[7]

Once the confidante of the king, the prince was now sliding down the same slippery slope as his brother. When his father fell ill and worries grew for the future of the monarchy, the Duke of York took his seat in the House of Lords and immediately began to press for his brother George's right to serve as Regent. As the press, public and politicians alike wrangled over who exactly should head the apparently inevitable Regency, William Pitt's Regency Bill was the hottest topic of debate. On 15 December 1788 Frederick rose in the Lords and made a speech which threw his support squarely behind the brother with whom he had shared virtually every waking moment and even a bedroom during their formative years. To many, Frederick was the more measured and self-controlled mouthpiece of the Prince of Wales, able to address the House of Lords on behalf of the brother who could not.

They had shared other things too. When he was just 19, the Prince of Wales enjoyed an intrigue with Madame Hardenburg, the wife of a Hanoverian minister. She put ideas of an elopement into his head and found herself swiftly dispatched back to Hanover as a result. Once there, she set her cap at Frederick instead and he admitted that, despite knowing of his brother's attachment to her, 'I desired no better fun' than a few moments alone with the lady. Unfortunately, in a rather comical turn of events the would-be lovers couldn't find an empty room in which to tryst, so Madame Hardenburg remained one shared interest that might have been.

But it suggested that Frederick and George weren't as different as George III might have hoped.

When he addressed the Lords, Frederick pointed out that the Prince of Wales would only accept the Regency if it was the will of the people and Parliament, but if he did so, he must be allowed to rule on his own terms. The thought that he would seek to wrest power from his father and hand it to his brother was abhorrent, said Frederick. 'My own debt of gratitude to the King is ample,' he told the hushed chamber, 'And when I forget it, or forsake him, may God forget and forsake me!'

As the Regency Bill was painstakingly debated and amended, Frederick was a constant presence at Westminster. At home the queen, already at her wit's end over her husband's illness, became ever more disillusioned with her elder sons. She was constantly looking for evidence of a plot to seize power and warned them, 'I most earnestly desire that neither [Wales] nor [Frederick] will make use of my name in any shape or upon any occasion whatsoever.'[8] As far as she was concerned, all they really cared about was power.

Though the Prince of Wales and the Duke of York were regular visitors to their ailing father at Kew, Charlotte was suspicious of their motives. Although she had always had a very respectful, if rather formal, relationship with her second son, she came to believe that Frederick's heartfelt wishes for the king's swift recovery were nothing but lip service and that behind the scenes, he would be agitating for his brother. In fact, Frederick was quite open in his belief that the Prince of Wales should be given control of both the country and the royal household. He could think of no better candidate. Things between Frederick and Charlotte eventually came to a head when they had a blazing row in 1789, prompting Frederick to declare that his mother and father were as deranged as one another.

The king's return to health ended any debate about the Regency, but at home things remained rocky. As Charlotte drew her daughters to her in a sheltered, unhappy cabal that would come to define their lives, she still refused to entertain any reconciliation with her eldest sons. Yet for the king, the presence of George and Frederick was the tonic he needed and regardless of what Charlotte might have wanted, he was delighted by their company. Just as her relationship with the Prince of Wales had been strained, now Charlotte's relationship with Frederick collapsed too. So bad did it get that she even tried to prevent the princes from visiting their father during his recuperation.

Despite her anger, Charlotte couldn't divert her husband's wish to see George and Frederick and much to her annoyance, they were eventually admitted to see the king. The 1st Earl of Minto, who chartered the comings and goings of the Regency Bill in his diaries, described the scene and the queen's influence over her ailing husband.

'The meeting was extremely affecting and affectionate on both sides. The King, when he came to the door of the room where [Wales and York] were, stopped and said he was not yet able to go in, and cried very much, but after a little pause he said he found himself better, and came in. He embraced them both with the greatest tenderness, and shed tears on their faces, and both the Princes were much touched with the scene. [...] The Queen was present, and walking to and fro in the room with a countenance and manner of great dissatisfaction; and the King every now and then went to her in a submissive and soothing sort of tone, for she has acquired the same sort of authority over him that Willis and his men have, and the King's mind is totally subdued and in a state of the greatest weakness and subjection.'[9]

Frederick's temper was always more level than that of his mother and brother and it was he who attempted to broker a peace between the warring factions. Whilst Charlotte railed against the Whigs who she believed had wished ill-health on her husband to smooth their favoured candidate's path to the Regency and their own path to power, Frederick tried to convince her that it was nothing of the sort. The Whigs hated the thought of the king recovering, she spat, because it meant that their own chance of government under the Prince of Wales would be snatched away. Despite Frederick's protestations that everyone, regardless of political persuasion, wished a speedy return to health for George III, his mother wasn't having it. Her refusal to invite the brothers to a concert given to celebrate her husband's recovery rocketed the feud towards its climax.

The furious queen wrote a letter to her sons in which she said that they could attend the concert if they absolutely had to, but she was at pains to point out that the event was actually intended as a thank you to the Tories who had supported the king through his travails. Since the princes were Whigs, said Charlotte, they might prefer to keep their distance. Ultimately it was the Duke of York who was able to diffuse the queen's anger and calm the troubled waters, but not before he had had a taste of his mother's temper. It was something to behold.

Lord Minto's diaries hold one more aside that is worth mentioning here. Frederick's lover around the time of the Regency crisis was Sarah, Countess of Tyrconnell. Lady Tyrconnell's husband was George Carpenter, 2nd Earl of Tyrconnell, and he relished the leverage he gained from having a wife who was so very, *very* close to the seat of power. When Frederick and Lady Tyrconnell's affair came to an end, the lady and her slighted family took their revenge at Westminster.

> '[The] best joke is, that not only has she been in fits on the occasion, but that both her *father* and her *husband* resent the rupture as an affront and an indignity put on *them* and on the *family*. They vote accordingly against us.'[10]

In the world of Georgian politics, which side of the bed you slept on could be as important as which side of the House you sat on.

The Duel

The Duke of York might have been the voice of reason during his sojourn in Germany and even the man who brokered a peace between the Prince of Wales and the queen, but even he wasn't above accepting a challenge. In 1789, when Frederick heard that the Duke of Richmond, who was Master of the Ordnance and a powerful political figure, had engineered the appointment of his nephew and heir, Charles Lennox, to the position of Lieutenant Colonel in the Coldstream Guards, Frederick was outraged. He was the commanding officer of the regiment and the fact that the Tory-supporting Lennox had been promoted without his knowledge or agreement left him incensed.

Whenever the Duke of York and the Prince of Wales weren't present at Daubigny's, their military club, Lennox openly criticised them at every opportunity. When somebody told Frederick what had been going on, he lamented that Lennox's sniping wasn't the behaviour of a gentleman. Each man felt that the other had affronted his honour, the Duke of York by calling into question Lennox's rank, Lennox by being critical of the princes. To make matters worse, the two men had a confrontation during a parade and Lennox offended '*all* MILITARY ETIQUETTE, by grossly questioning his SUPERIOR at the very *head* of his REGIMENT.'[11] Frederick, mindful of reputation and honour, accepted Lennox's offer of a duel with pistols to settle the matter.

Lennox and Frederick met on Wimbledon Common on 26 May 1789 with their seconds, the Earl of Winchilsea and Lord Rawdon. Lennox brought a carriage loaded with bags in case he killed the duke and needed to make a swift escape, whilst Frederick arrived in borrowed clothes so as not to alert the household at Carlton House to his dawn departure. They took twelve paces then turned. Lennox fired a bullet that grazed the duke's hair but even though he escaped death literally by a whisker, Frederick didn't pull the trigger. When Lennox asked why Frederick hadn't fired, Rawdon explained on the duke's behalf that he'd never had any intention of doing so. Frederick wished his opponent no harm and had accepted the duel merely to protect his honour and give the Lieutenant Colonel satisfaction. On behalf of Lennox, Winchilsea asked if the duke would now confirm that he considered Lennox to be a man of honour and courage. Frederick, however, would confirm no such thing.

He came to Wimbledon simply to give Lennox satisfaction, he reiterated, and if Lennox hadn't received it, then they would take their twelve paces again.

Perhaps wisely, Lennox turned down the opportunity to replay the duel and the party broke up. This wasn't the end of the matter though. Mindful of how upset the royal family would be when they inevitably learned of the duel, Frederick knew that some damage limitation might be needed. Since Winchilsea was one of the king's lords of the bedchamber and Winchilsea's mother was none other than that old retainer, Lady Charlotte Finch, he knew that the chances of keeping the matter under wraps were scant. It was for this reason that he hastened from Wimbledon to Windsor, ready to assure his parents that he had lived to fight another day.

As Frederick related the story of the duel to the king and queen, George III gaped in horror at his son's admission that the ball had come close enough to part the curls of his hair. Queen Charlotte, however, was rather less troubled. She listened impassively to his account then declared that the duke had brought the whole sorry matter upon himself. It was all his fault, she said, and he had been the aggressor throughout.

It was, however, an important moment in the public life of the Duke of York. His support for the Prince of Wales over the Regency Bill had damaged his public standing but Frederick's cool, brave and honourable conduct during the duel did much to restore his popularity. What it didn't do, of course, was put any money into his swiftly depleting coffers.

Royal Wedding

Frederick's income was certainly far from meagre, but since he shared a love of gambling and high living with his brothers, it was bound to be inadequate. Of course, one way to make a quick lump sum was to take a rich bride and claim the dowry she'd bring with her. Though Frederick's affair with the married Lady Tyrconnell had once burned so bright that he had thrown the Duchess of Gordon out of the supper room at the Pantheon for being critical of her, it was over in the space of twelve short months. Even if the affair had lasted, it wouldn't have done much for Frederick's financial prospects because the lady was already a wife. For a time, he wondered about marrying the widowed Duchess of Rutland, but she had plenty of other lovers too and the Prince of Wales talked Frederick out of the possibly unwise match.

A bride was one sure-fire way of making money, but Frederick would rather have been heading to war. He petitioned the king to send him abroad on military business. In Europe sabres were rattling and Prussia was readying itself for a possible war with Russia over disputed Turkish territory. George agreed that Frederick could return to Prussia and see if there might be a place for him with the Prussian army. However, by the time he arrived, the danger had passed, and Prussia had no need of his services. There was another duty he could perform though, and he wrote to his father from Berlin to remind him that, not so long ago, the king had expressed a wish that at least one of his sons should marry. Frederick wrote:

'From that moment this idea has never been out of my thoughts [...] The only delicacy which I felt upon this subject was from not being informed of the sentiments of my elder brother, the Prince of Wales, but having taken an opportunity of speaking to him very openly, he declared to me repeatedly his disinclination at present to matrimony and his wish that I should marry. I had therefore intended to have asked your Majesty's leave to have come to Germany this autumn, had nothing extraordinary happened. The appearance of an immediate war which hurried me away from England made me for a time lose sight of my objects, but the instant the probability subsided I began to consider again of my first plan.

I think it my duty to confess to your Majesty that from the first time I saw the King of Prussia's eldest daughter, the Princess Frederique [sic], she was not wholly indifferent to me, and though I did not think it right at that moment to encourage any hope concerning her, not being acquainted with your majesty's sentiments, yet the very instant I knew them, she was always my object. Having had an opportunity during my stay here to see her and to enquire very particularly after her, I am perfectly convinced that her person and disposition are such as to make me perfectly happy. Allow me therefore, Sir, to entreat you as my father and my King to grant me your consent to marry her, and to obtain her for me of the King her father. Indeed, Sir, all my future comfort depends upon it. This resolution of mine is not one taken in a hurry or from passion alone but after thorough and mature consideration.'[12]

Thankfully for his parents, Frederick didn't follow his elder brother's lead and make an illegal marriage. Instead he did things by the book and sought a marriage to Princess Frederica Charlotte of Prussia, the cousin who had caught his eye during his trip to the continent. Frederica Charlotte was the only child of Frederick William II of Prussia and his first wife, Elisabeth Christine of Brunswick-Lüneberg[13]. She hadn't seen her mother since she was two years old, when Frederick William and Elisabeth Christine had divorced and the latter had been placed under house arrest for seven decades in retaliation for her extra-marital affairs. Before we judge her too harshly though, it's worth noting that Frederick William had enjoyed plenty of affairs and even bigamous marriages of his own.

The little girl was raised by her great-aunt and great-uncle, Elisabeth Christine of Brunswick-Wolfenbüttel-Bevern and Frederick the Great. She was seen as the safest of safe bets for the Duke of York. Despite her scandalous parents, Frederica Charlotte's upbringing had been one of the utmost respectability, and she ticked all the boxes on the royal wish list. She was a German Protestant and at 24 years old, very definitely of childbearing age. Since the Prince of Wales had yet to make his own *legal* marriage, it was vital that Frederick start producing heirs as quickly as possible and with Frederica Charlotte, that looked like a distinct possibility. Even Queen Charlotte, famously critical when it came to the possible spouses of her children, approved of the harmless princess. Just as Frederick had wished, consent was duly given. In London, the king and queen were delighted by the promised match. Their eldest son had shown no inclination to marry yet here was the spare seeking betrothal to the daughter of a reigning king, no less. They could ask for nothing more.

'His Majesty in Council was this Day pleased to declare His Consent to a Contract of Matrimony between His Royal Highness The Princess Frederique, Charlotte, Ulrique, Catherine of Prussia, eldest Daughter of His Majesty The King of Prussia, which Consent his Majesty has also caused to be signified under the Great Seal.'[14]

The union was agreed, and Frederick remained in Berlin, where the couple was to be married before their planned return to England. The wedding festivities were immense and amongst those present were Princes William and Augustus. The ceremony took place on the evening of 29 September 1791 in the White Hall of Charlottenburg Palace, kicking off celebrations that went on for days.

On 30 September 1791, Lord Malmesbury wrote to the Prince of Wales to inform him that the ceremony had passed without incident.

'[The Duke of York] has commanded me to acquaint you, that He was married yesterday evening, & at the same time to express to Yr Royal Highness His feelings of gratitude & affection for the kind and Fraternal manner in which you have behav'd towards him on this occasion.

[…]

I Have had the pleasure to see this morning both the duke and dutchess [sic] of York, perfectly well & happy beyond description.'[15]

And for a time, they were.

Gripped by royal wedding fever, the public couldn't wait to meet the new Duchess of York. As the people waited for Frederick and Frederica Charlotte to make their first official appearance, the press was filled with reports from Berlin of the glittering celebrations and the lady who was making her way to England.

'Her Royal Highness the present Duchess of York is short in stature; her symmetry, however, is exact.

[…]

Her countenance resembles in style of feature, her august Parent's – the eye, like his, is full and mild – the mouth, small, and not projecting, the chin sweetly turned, and, as a physiognomist would remark, indicatory of sensibility and fine temper. Her complexion is fair, clear, and healthy; the hair approaching to flaxen. The nose is by no means well-shaped, it swells at the extremity, and inclines upward.

How her Royal Highness has discharged the filial duties, Berlin from every tongue can testify – there is accordingly the happiest presumption, that the spousal will be discharged with the same steadiness of affection, and fedulity of attention.

The accomplishments of this amiable Princess are many – her taste is pure and perfect.

[…]

Perhaps greater regret Berlin will never know, than when her Royal Highness quits it for Britain.'[16]

The couple left Berlin in October and travelled through Germany, paying visits along the way before they finally sailed for England as October drew to a close. On their arrival in London the duke and duchess were married again, this time in a glittering ceremony at Buckingham House. This second ceremony sealed the marriage under the auspices of the Royal Marriages Act.

The fascination with Frederica Charlotte was widespread and as so many celebrities discover nowadays, her looks were of utmost importance. Yet it wasn't the new duchess' face that the public couldn't get enough of, it was her feet. Frederica Charlotte was a very slight woman and her feet were famously tiny, measuring less than six inches in length. Their daintiness became a talking point and soon souvenir hunters were snapping up replicas of her shoes. The Duchess of York's little feet were famously caricatured by Gillray in his work, *Fashionable Contrasts; – or – The Duchess's little Shoe yielding to the Magnitude of the Duke's Foot*, which was published by Hannah Humphrey on 24 January 1792.

The cartoon depicts Duke and Duchess of York caught in a compromising position. Her tiny feet are clad in ornate jewelled slippers, whilst his large and long feet are between hers, as though the couple are wrapped in a passionate embrace. The illustration was a hit and prints sold by the bucket load as the public laughed along with Gillray at the obsession with Frederica Charlotte's feet.

The marriage had the hoped-for financial result too. Now he was a husband the Duke's income was duly increased by Parliament and he pocketed a dowry of 100,000 crowns from his wife's family. The Yorks made their home at Oatlands Park, where a Tudor palace had once stood, and they ploughed a fortune into their new estate, determined to live a regal life.

Though Frederick had lobbied for the marriage, things went sour at a spectacular speed. Three years after the marriage there were still no children and the king and queen accepted that the chance of their second son producing an heir were virtually zero. Though never officially separated, the couple were now no more than friends.

A Military Man

As Frederick's marriage was crumbling, across the sea France was in a state of turmoil all of its own. No sooner had Louis XVI been guillotined than the governing Convention declared war on Britain. Within months that had been extended to include the Dutch Republic. The time had finally come for Frederick, now promoted to general, to prove his mettle in the field.

With French armies poised to invade the Dutch Republic and overthrow the ruling House of Orange, Pitt agreed that Frederick should be sent to Flanders to command the Dutch troops there. Although they were ostensibly under the command of the Hereditary Prince William of Orange, the 21-year-old was vastly inexperienced and would benefit from the presence of a more worldly pair of hands. The obvious candidate was the Duke of York, who might not have seen front line action, but had been well prepared to do so. The man who had commanded a regiment now held the British Expeditionary Forces and Hanoverian army in the palm of his hand. He was just a few months short of his thirtieth birthday.

Frederick was in almost constant contact with the king during his campaign on the continent. He kept his father appraised of the situation in Flanders and proved himself time and again to be a more than capable soldier. Perhaps his most notable victory came at the Siege of Valenciennes in the summer of 1793, when General Jean-Henri-Becays Ferrand's French army, beaten into submission by the Coburg forces, took refuge in the fortified town of Valenciennes. Prince Josias of Saxe-Coburg-Saalfeld entrusted Frederick with the command of his armies and charged him with besieging and capturing the stronghold, with Austrian assistance.

In Great Britain, Parliament viewed the decision with dismay. For all his studies, the Duke of York was a British prince and the British troops were hardly masters of siege warfare. Yet the duke proved himself once again and under his command, Valenciennes fell. The Duke of York was hailed as a hero by both his comrades and the people of the besieged town. As Frederick concluded talks with the surrendering army 'a very ludicrous circumstance happened [and] the Director of the Theatre at Valenciennes deserted out of the town, and he said on purpose to enquire what play I chose to have acted at Valenciennes tonight, and he of himself offered to act *Richard Cour de Lion*.' It was a triumph to be savoured.[17]

Yet Frederick was to find that life as a soldier could bring defeat as well as victory.

After their triumph at Valenciennes, the allies continued their route through France. Their opponents were on the backfoot and Frederick's letters are full of cautious optimism about the outcome of the fighting. The troops were in good spirits and so was he, but at Dunkirk things were set to change.

In September 1793, military commanders, including the Duke of York, believed that the time was right to mount an assault on Paris itself. At home in Britain, however, Pitt and Henry Dundas, the Minister for War, disagreed. Instead they pressed for the allies to march on Dunkirk. Though it meant that they would be heading to the coast rather than further inland, victory at Dunkirk would provide Britain with a valuable base in Europe as well as a potential bargaining chip when it came to what looked like an inevitable allied victory. Frederick doubted the wisdom of such a decision, but he was a dutiful soldier and obeyed his orders whatever they might be. Despite his wishes to capitalise on the allied advantage and march on Paris, he followed Pitt's orders and led his 20,000 strong force towards Dunkirk. With French defences battered and the attack on Dunkirk unexpected, it looked like an easy victory. It was to be anything but.

In Paris, the election of Pierre Louis Prieur and Lazare Carnot brought a much-needed injection of new strategic blood to the Committee of Public Safety. Mindful of the sorry state of the military in Dunkirk and the morale of citizens there who looked likely to surrender, they shored up the under-defended town with tens of thousands of troops gathered from across France. Still it looked as though an allied victory was on the cards, but things went unexpectedly and badly wrong for the duke's forces. They simply weren't equipped to break a siege and with French ships blocking access to the port, no siege machines could be brought into Dunkirk. If an allied win was to be secured, naval support was vital. Instead it was conspicuously absent and when French commanders opened Dunkirk's sluices, the British camp was turned into a swamp. Disease was rife and morale plummeted. To make matters worse, French prisoners who had been released after the fall of Valenciennes on the understanding that they wouldn't re-join and fight against the British did just that, further bolstering numbers. It was a mess and the Duke of York knew it.

In the early days of September, the French redoubled their efforts to force the defeat of Frederick's forces. After a brutal toe-to-toe battle the attack was repelled, but at great cost to both sides. All around them the coalition was embattled, with Hanoverian troops forced into retreat until the once apparently unstoppable force had been effectively carved up. With no other choice, the duke withdrew into Belgium, abandoning a fortune in military baggage in the retreat. A few days later the British fleet finally arrived, far too late to be of any use whatsoever. Had the fleet arrived earlier as the duke had expected, the outcome would have been completely different. As it was, the victory was claimed by the French.

Frederick was shaken by the retreat but he told his elder brother that '[my] only comfort is that none of the blame of this shamefull [sic] retreat can be thrown upon me, and that it is known that I have done everything in my power to prevent it.'[18] The soldiers in France, whose commanders

– including Frederick - had warned of the dangers of pushing to take Dunkirk, had been let down by their masters in Parliament. Frederick himself took small comfort in that and the knowledge that 'Whatever opinion your Majesty may be pleased to form upon my conduct, want of zeal I trust will never be laid to my charge.'[19]

He was still the favourite, after all.

The Grand Old Duke of York

The Duke of York had pressed to march on Paris rather than Dunkirk and his advice had gone unheeded. Now Holy Roman Emperor Francis II arrived to oversee the Allied forces but once again, the duke found that his strategies differed from those of the high command. Yet Frederick, a well-drilled and loyal soldier, would follow the emperor's orders regardless of his own opinions on them, because following orders was what he had been raised to do. Against his better judgment he advanced on Tourcoing, in the very far north of France, supposedly as an overture for the onslaught that would force the French out of Flanders.

The Hanoverian-Habsburg-British coalition under the command of Prince Josias of Saxe-Coburg-Saalfeld and the Duke of York was to face the massed forces of France, led by General Joseph Souham. The coalition battle plans relied on the encirclement of the Republican Army, but the Battle of Tourcoing in May 1794 didn't go according to plan. Though the French were outnumbered, they had the strategic advantage as the coalition forces found their advance hampered and slowed by the territory. By the end of the battle, France had claimed the victory and when Frederick was separated from his army, he came perilously close to falling into enemy hands. The duke galloped away with the French cavalry in pursuit and escaped only by wading through a brook to safety. It was an ignominious end to a disastrous battle.

The infamous Flanders campaign provided one of many potential origins for the nursery rhyme, *The Grand Old Duke of York*. In fact, the earliest versions of the rhyme were certainly not contemporary to Frederick's lifetime, even if it became his lasting impact on the popular consciousness. Frederick and his 10,000 men might have marched here there and everywhere but in the final reckoning, they had achieved little of note in Flanders. Coalition losses at Tourcoing were nearly double those of the French.

When the emperor returned to Vienna, he found that many of his officers requested permission to join him. Morale was plummeting and though Frederick was ostensibly in command of the coalition troops, by the summer of 1794, their effectiveness was vastly reduced. With the withdrawal of the Austrian forces, it seemed that all hope of victory was lost. The duke was given reinforcements as autumn fell but it was too little, too late. The troops he received were ill-disciplined and untrained, certainly no match for a French army that was already buoyed by its successes in the preceding months. With the allies in retreat or ready to throw in the towel, Frederick's poor opinion of the Dutch soldiers was soon extended to the Austrians and Hanoverians too. According to Frederick's brother, Prince Ernest, who was also fighting with the coalition, these feelings went both ways, and he wrote to the Prince of Wales on 1 December 1794 to tell him that 'the Duke has lost all his reputation with the Austrians'[20]. After so many defeats, they had simply lost the will to go on.

> 'I am commanded to signify to Your Royal Highness His Majesty's pleasure that You should take the earliest opportunity of returning to England, leaving the command of His Majesty's British Forces in the hands of such British Officer as may be next in Seniority to Your Royal Highness after furnishing him with such information and Instructions as Your Royal Highness may judge to be necessary for his guidance.'[21]

By the time the duke was recalled to England in November 1794 by the above letter from Henry Dundas, the campaign had proved catastrophic for the coalition. Luxembourg surrendered in June 1795 and with the end of hostilities and the French seizure of the Austrian Netherlands, the Holy Roman Empire was dealt a crippling blow. Britain, meanwhile, lost her close European allies in the Dutch Republic. At home, the duke was attacked as a boy playing at being a soldier and the wrong man for a job that had required an experienced and clear-headed strategist, yet this was unfair to him. Whilst it's true that he lacked the experience that might have been valuable when it came to the moment of reckoning, he was ill-served by his masters both in government and in the field. Yet in Frederick's lengthy letters to his father, the two agreed that Austria's refusal to abandon its system of cordons, by which they had one long but stretched line of defence rather than a concentrated defensive force, played a key part in the outcome of the battle. At home, the caricaturists and critics painted Frederick as a man who had been given rank due to his family, rather than because he had any real skill, but to lay the blame for the failure of the coalition campaign entirely at the door of the Duke of York is unjust.

One thing that Frederick did take away from his experience in Flanders was the poor state of the British army. It was something that later, as commander-in-chief, he sought to address through a widespread programme of reform. Never again would the force face such a defeat, Frederick promised, and he would do all he could to ensure that things changed.

Commander-in-Chief

Whilst Frederick had not excelled as he might have hoped when it came to the battlefield, one thing he had realised without a doubt was that the vast and unwieldy army was ripe for reform. In 1795 the king promoted his son to the position of field marshal then, three years later, the Duke of York was made commander-in-chief of the army. He was to replace Lord Amherst, who was by then in his late seventies and would die just two years later. Though Amherst had been distinguished in his day, his reappointment in 1793 had been the start of a tenure in which the army slid at a rapid rate into the worst of habits. As the Prince of Wales looked on enviously at his brother's military position, the duke settled into his new job with admirable speed.

Though we might expect Frederick's appointment to attract accusations of nepotism, in fact, the duke's promotion was welcomed. From his offices above Horse Guards, he led a dynamic programme of military reform, working ten hours a day to tirelessly bring about the changes that he believed were crucial to drag the army up to standard. Frederick was hardly a man of extensive military experience despite his frontline service, yet there was something about him that appealed to the rank and file soldiers under his command. He was known for his dynamic and steady – at least compared to his older brother – character and when he was made commander-in-chief, Frederick swiftly proved that he intended to make a splash in his new position. In fact, his initiatives earned him the nickname, *the Soldier's Friend*, with some even adding an additional stanza to *God Save the King* in his honour.

> 'When rous'd by war's alarms,
> Britons will rush to arms,
> And guard their King;
> Their land they will defend,
> While shouts the welkin rend,
> Of YORK, the Soldier's friend,
> And GEORGE our King.'

Frederick undertook tours of inspection to establish just how poor the standard of the British army had become. The duke was shocked by what he discovered, particularly regarding the widespread disregard for the *Rules and Regulations for the Formations, Field Exercises and Movements of H.M. Forces*, which had been issued on the command of George III in 1792. One of his first acts as commander-in-chief was to insist that the instructions contained in the manual be followed to the letter. Drill, which had become slovenly and ineffective, was emphasised as vital to the creation of a disciplined fighting force to be reckoned with. He had inherited an army that was at war with France, after all, and had personally witnessed the disastrous campaign in the Low Countries. Few knew better than the Duke of York that, should France invade Britain, then the country was ill-prepared to deal with such a threat.

Although Frederick's status inevitably meant that he certainly enjoyed the best conditions that army life had to offer during his active service, one of the things that he was most determined to tackle was the broken purchase system. This system allowed rich men to buy themselves a prestigious military rank and enjoy all the respect and privilege that came with it. Should his chosen regiment be posted abroad and the gentleman – heaven forbid – face the prospect of actually fighting, he merely bought his way into another regiment that would allow him to continue his comfortable existence at home. Perhaps the most famous example was Beau Brummell's decision to quit to 10th Light Dragoons when they were sent to Manchester. After all, said the famously fashion-obsessed Brummell, he had 'not enlisted for foreign service'.

This system of buying commissions also meant that promotion didn't have to be earned on merit and ability. Instead, one could simply buy one's way into power. Stopping this outright would have been like trying to hold back the tide, but the duke did what he could to tackle the more obvious abuses. He clamped down on the *anything goes* approach of some officers, who were rarely to be found at their posts, and increased the promotions made on merit. As Frederick found out to his cost later, however, this was a system that could still be abused.

Having witnessed life in the British army firsthand, Frederick greatly reduced the use of corporal punishment for minor offences and became determined to improve morale wherever possible. This, along with notoriously poor conditions for new recruits, had been a major stumbling block when it came to filling out the ranks, and the Duke of York knew it. He ruled that corporal punishment should be used for only the most serious offences and he made it clear he was happy to personally meet soldiers who had made allegations of abusive treatment. Yet all of this was pointless if there were no new recruits to enjoy the improved system of army discipline. Aware that the ranks needed to see an improvement in all aspects of life, the Duke of York also put in place measures to modernise uniforms and barracks, improve rations and even to increase pay for privates.

To ensure that soldiers could continue to serve for as long as possible, Frederick took a personal interest in military hospitals. During his tenure, he established a new system of inspections and introduced measurable standards for hygiene and cleanliness, including new fumigation techniques. There was even a programme of vaccination against smallpox, which was made available to every British soldier regardless of where he was stationed.

All of this came not a moment too soon. On the continent, Napoleon was scattering his opponents before him, bringing the threat of a French invasion ever closer. In late 1796 a French fleet headed towards Ireland on the first stage of what looked like an imminent invasion, but the weather was on the side of Great Britain and the fleet was beaten back by severe storms. With Austria crumbling under French assault all attention turned to Britain, whose defence rested on the Royal Navy at sea and the army on land. Now more than ever, Britain needed to know that she was protected not by lazy, ill-disciplined good for nothings, but by a loyal and well-drilled fighting force. When Britain and France faced off this time, there were no allies left to call upon.

And just when it seemed as though things couldn't get any worse, trouble erupted in the ranks. Members of the Royal Navy understood it was effectively them, not the army, that had kept Britain defended from the French threat. When the new commander-in-chief requested a pay increase for the army and Parliament accepted it, some naval men were outraged. Where was their pay rise, they asked, especially given their tireless defence of the country? Perhaps inevitably the result was a mutiny, though one which was short-lived. Not so long ago one might have expected the ill-disciplined and dissatisfied men of the army to follow the example of their nautical comrades, but no such thing happened. Instead the men stayed loyal to the commander-in-chief who had pledged to improve their lot.

The Duke of York's reforms might only have been in their infancy at this dire moment in the history of George III's realm, but it was enough. The army stood firm, ready to defend the country should the invasion fleet land, just as it was ready to defend British interests across the globe.

Their first great test came in 1798 when the Napoleonic armies turned their sights on Egypt as the first stop on a campaign against British India. Following weeks of fruitless pursuit, Nelson caught up with the French fleet in Aboukir Bay and after a ferocious battle, laid waste to it. The tide of war was turning and in Britain, where high taxes and deprivation had led to outbursts of dissent on the streets, the atmosphere of seething anger began to turn into one of hope. Mindful of what had happened in France not so long ago, Pitt was willing to make the most of the newly effective army to control the populace, but the victory in Egypt fortunately transformed the mood.

When Britain and Russia agreed their alliance in 1799, the fightback of the Second Coalition began in earnest. Austria set aside her peace with France and joined the coalition alongside the Ottoman Empire and other members. In Europe, the comeback had begun. The Duke of York, not a man to sit behind his desk whilst his men went to war, was determined to be a part of it.

Frederick joined the Anglo–Russian invasion of Holland in 1799, ready to make his mark. Though the campaign began well when three Dutch ships were captured, it went rapidly downhill from there.

The Duke of York arrived in Holland at the head of a force numbering 30,000 men with a further 18,000 troops provided by Russia. The decision to award him command was a clear signal that his campaign in Flanders several years earlier had been forgiven and that, whatever the outcome, it hadn't left a stain on the Duke of York's reputation. Likewise, since it was intended that the outcome of this battle would be the restoration of the House of Orange, exiled since the Batavian Revolution of 1795, Henry Dundas noted:

'This is certainly a command for the King's son, and I cannot help thinking that with a view to future connection it is desirable that a Prince of the Blood should have a chief part in the deliverance of Holland, and the re-establishment of the House of Orange. Besides his Royal Highness being on the spot and having the influence which it is said he has with the Prince of Orange, may be of essential use in the future.'[22]

Dundas spoke for Pitt's administration, which was confident that the outcome of the Helder campaign would be a British victory. But they had reckoned without the weather.

Fierce conditions meant that Frederick's forces couldn't land until late August, by which time their opponents had received ample word that trouble was on its way. Despite this, the British managed to inflict heavy losses on the Dutch at Callantsoog. The Batavian Navy, though fighting with the French, was of questionable loyalty already so when the Hereditary Prince of Orange joined with the coalition forces, those sailors loyal to the House of Orange finally declared themselves not for the republic, but the monarchy. To ram the point home the coalition ships were carrying Orange flags and propaganda, a reminder of all that had been lost by capitulation to the French.

In what has become known as the Vlieter incident, the Batavian fleet under the command of Rear-Admiral Samuel Story mutinied and handed itself over to the British without a single shot being fired. The Hereditary Prince of Orange visited the ships to personally thank those who had turned against the new republic in support of the old regime.

Unfortunately, the civilian population of North Holland didn't share the opinion of the mutineers. The Batavian army had no intention of following their naval comrades into surrender. Rather than press its advantage, the British navy waited for the Duke of York and his armies to arrive, and this was to prove a fatal mistake.

The combined coalition land forces were nearly double those of the Franco–Batavian army, but from the start things went badly. Frederick drew up a plan in which four columns would overwhelm the Franco-Batavian army, but the Russian column started too early. Rather than wait until dawn, they moved out in the early hours and as a result, in the firefight that followed many coalition soldiers were lost to friendly fire. A second column, this one led by General Dundas and Frederick, had reckoned without bodies of water that were impassable because their opponents had dismantled all the bridges. The third column suffered similar setbacks, though it did manage to inflict some heavy losses on the Batavian forces.

The fourth column, however, had more success. They arrived at Hoorn unopposed and had succeeded in occupying the city when they received word to retreat, as the other columns had been unsuccessful in their aims. No territory was won, and many lives were lost on both sides. This campaign provided the second possible origin for the comical tale of *The Grand Old Duke of York*.

In the coalition camp, morale dipped as terrible weather swept across the land. Though there were some hopes that the Dutch people might rise up in revolution, in reality, things were going from bad to worse. Eventually, with all hope of success lost, the duke signed the Convention of Alkmaar. This allowed the Anglo-Russian coalition to leave Holland on condition that some 8,000 French prisoners of war were released. The duke felt that he had no choice in the matter and believed that, should he attempt to fight on, the losses would be catastrophic.

'Knowing the loss which we must have sustained of most our artillery and the whole of our rear guard at the Helder,' he wrote to his father on 21 October 1799, 'I thought myself duty bound to sacrifice all personal and private feelings, which I cannot conceal from your Majesty were very tried, to what I judged the advantage of your Majesty's service and the saving of many valuable men's lives.'[23]

And what of George III? He didn't rail and complain at the costly retreat but instead took it with a rather more worldly air. It was all part of being a king.

> 'I was never very sanguine as to the success of the attempt on Holland, and for some time, have certainly felt that the earlier it was given up the better. Indeed, had the people of that country been hearty it might have ended better, but would ever have been most hazardous. I therefore approve of the suspension of hostilities even at the giving up 8000 prisoners of the French.'[24]

Though the agreement ensured that the allied forces would live to fight another day, it also confirmed that the Duke of York wasn't cut out for active military command. He was to remain at his desk for the rest of his career.

Upon his return to Horse Guards, the duke continued with his reforming zeal. Rich with new experience from the front line, he determined that in order for officers to properly train the men under them, then those officers must first be properly trained themselves. This led to the creation of the Royal Military College and laid the foundations for what would eventually become Sandhurst. Alongside these initiatives was the creation of an establishment where the orphans of military personnel could be cared for. The Royal Military Asylum for Children of Soldiers of the Regular Army employed a system whereby children older than 13 served as tutors to the younger pupils. As the children grew into adults, they either enlisted in the army or were apprenticed to a trade. It was unlike anything the English army had seen before, and was modelled on the Royal Hibernian Military School in Dublin. The opportunities the Royal Asylum offered to children who might previously have faced uncertain futures can't be underestimated.

Frederick laid the first stone at Chelsea in 1801 and two years later, the asylum opened. At its height it housed a thousand boys and 500 girls, and Frederick took an interest in it throughout his life. Not for him the cossetted life of the Prince of Wales. Having served on the front line and seen conditions at their most dire, he was determined that the children of those who had fallen would receive the care they deserved.

Yet despite his finer qualities, the Duke of York retained a love for the sort of dissolute living that had got his elder brother into trouble. In 1803, he made a decision that was to have a catastrophic effect on the career that he valued so highly.

Mrs Clarke

Mary Anne Clarke seemed to come from nowhere. Like so many other courtesans before her, she deliberately smudged her origins in order to create a tantalising smokescreen for the men who fell at her feet. What little we know of her early life is unreliable, but it would seem that she was born in London in the mid-1770s to an unnamed mother and a tradesman father, who died when she was still a young girl. Mary's mother remarried quickly, this time to a print worker who gave his young stepdaughter errands to run on his behalf. Mary learned to read and write and her intelligence, combined with a ready wit and street smarts, saw her married at the age of 17 to Joseph Clarke, the son of a wealthy man. If Mary hoped that marriage would be her ticket to the easy life, she was sorely mistaken. Joseph was an unfaithful drunkard who drove his family – including the two children he and Mary had – into bankruptcy. Yet Mary wasn't going to follow her man all the way to debtor's prison. She packed her bags, gathered up her children and set off for a new life.

Though Mary later claimed that she'd been a famous actress, she made her name as a celebrated courtesan and it was only a matter of time before her path crossed that of the royal princes. In 1803 Mary reached the peak of her career when Frederick, Duke of York, installed her as his official mistress. Thanks to Frederick's money the one-time errand girl from the backstreets could enjoy a celebrity lifestyle at last, presiding over dozens of staff as the chatelaine of 18 Gloucester Place.

As befits a royal mistress, Mary was given money by the duke as and when she needed it, but it was never quite enough to meet her needs. If Mary wanted the lifestyle that she believed she deserved, she needed a side hustle. Her affair with the commander-in-chief gave her just the opportunity she was looking for.

As part of his clampdown on unsuitable men gaining promotions, the Duke of York personally approved the lists of every soldier who was due to advance in the ranks. However, although the duke had taken a close interest in the matter of reform, he didn't have time to cross reference each and every name on the lists. Instead, he simply signed them off and the promotions went through. What he didn't know was that Mary had been selling cut-rate commissions of her own to ambitious and enterprising soldiers who knew they could save a fortune by going via Mrs Clarke rather than the official, expensive channels.

All Mary had to do was add the name of the gentleman to the list and since she often wrote them out for the duke anyway, he didn't even notice a discrepancy in the handwriting. Mary's little earner came to an end in 1806 when her relationship with Frederick fizzled out, but she wasn't about to go quietly. She threatened to publish tell-all memoirs unless the duke kept on funding her lifestyle, and he agreed. However, Frederick couldn't keep up the payments forever and in 1808 he cut off Mary's line of credit. That same year Major Denis Hogan published a memoir in which he categorically stated that bargain commissions could be purchased from Mary Anne Clarke.

'It has been often observed to me by *connoisseurs*, that I should have had no reason to complain, if I had proceeded in the *proper way* to seek promotion. But what is meant by the *proper way*? I applied to the Duke of York, because he was commander-in-chief. To his royal highness I was directed by the king's orders to apply; and with these orders alone I felt it consistent with my duty as an officer, and my honour as a gentleman, to comply. But if any other person had been the substitute of the Duke of York, I should have made my application to that person. If a [...] *Clarke* [...] had been invested by his majesty with the office of commander-in-chief, to that person I should have applied; nay, if it had pleased his majesty to confer upon a female the *direct command* of the army, I should have done my duty, in applying to the legal depositary of power: but to none other should I condescend to apply; for I scorn undue influence, and feel incapable of enjoying any object, however intrinsically valuable, that should be procured by such means.'[25]

And things were about to get worse.

In the wake of Major Hogan's claims, Colonel Gwyllym Lloyd Wardle MP recalled spending an afternoon at Mrs Clarke's residence when the Duke of York's carriage arrived. Fearful of discovery, Colonel Wardle dived beneath the sofa and observed as one of Frederick's aides-de-camp openly discussed the sale of commissions with Mary. Wardle was certain that this meant the duke was complicit in the sorry business and he was ready to make it public.

On 20 January 1809, Wardle introduced a motion in the House of Commons calling for an inquest into the sale of commissions by the Duke of York and Mary Anne Clarke. When the inquest opened, it was the hottest ticket in London, starring the most infamous leading lady of them all.

'Mrs. CLARKE, when she appeared before the House of Commons on Wednesday, was dressed as if she had been going out to an evening party, in a light blue silk gown and coat, edged with white fur, and a white muff. On her head she wore a white cap or veil which at no time was let down over her face. In size she is rather small, and she does not seem to be particularly well made. She has a fair, clear, smooth skin, and lively blue eyes, but her features are not handsome. Her nose is rather short and turning up, and her teeth are very indifferent; yet she has an appearance of great vivacity of manners, but is not said to be a well-bred or accomplished woman. She appears to be about thirty-five yearse [sic] of age, and probably has recommended herself more by her agreeable and lively spirit than by her beauty. When first she came into the House [of Commons] she was very pale; on her second appearance the colour flushed into her face, which was like vermillion; but she seemed not at all daunted or embarrassed at any time.'[26]

For a fortnight the Commons and the public raked through the bones of Mary and Frederick's relationship. Mary sang like a bird, sparkling on the stand as she charmed the men who had intended to humble her. The Duke of York was entirely aware of the commission sales, she claimed, because he set the prices and took the lion's share of the profits. Frederick, who had largely enjoyed the approval of the public whilst the Prince of Wales had faced their ire, was now held in the same contempt as the heir to the throne. What sort of men were these, asked the people, who would watch their father suffer as they dragged the reputation of the royal house through the mud? Far from caring about reform and reward where it was deserved, they now believed that the Duke of York loved nothing more than lining his own pockets.

The king was kept abreast of the proceedings by Spencer Perceval, who assured him that Mary and Wardle's claims were false and that the pair were motivated by malice and political opposition, but not everyone agreed. At worst, the duke was corrupt, at best, a fool who had been duped by his mistress. As Lord Temple pointed out though, foolishness could not be a defence, 'though he could not concur in opinion that distinct charges of corruption or connivance were proved against the Duke of York, [he] appeared deeply criminal in allowing an intriguing mistress to interfere in his royal duties'[27]. Lest there be any doubt about the gravity of the charges, Temple 'thought it incumbent therefore on his Royal Highness to resign the command of the army.' William Wilberforce likewise condemned Frederick and damned 'the immoral tendency which the licentious conduct of his Royal Highness might have toward corrupting the public morals.'[28]

Westminster and Britain were in uproar, divided on whether the Duke of York was an innocent dupe or a conniving wrongdoer, but he would at least be given the chance to clear his name. As a prince, Frederick wasn't required to face the House and was permitted instead to submit a letter in his own defence. It was a heartfelt plea, but it would be up to Parliament to decide whether it was believed.

'I have waited with the greatest anxiety until the Committee of Inquiry had closed its examination, and I now hope it will not be deemed improper in me to address a letter to the House of

Commons, through you, on the subject. I observe, with the deepest concern, that in the course of the inquiry that has been gone into, my name has been coupled with transactions of the most criminal and disgraceful nature; and I must always lament a connection that has exposed my honour and my character to such unmerited animadversions. With respect to any concern in such transactions, I now, ON THE HONOUR OF A PRINCE, most solemnly assert MY ENTIRE INNOCENCE. I deny, not only any participation in, or connivance at, those transactions, but also the least knowledge or consciousness of their existence. I hope that the House of Commons will not, upon such evidence as has been produced, adopt any proceeding prejudicial to my character and honour; but if upon such testimony, the House of Commons should think my innocence questionable, I claim from them the justice of not being condemned without a trial, nor tried without those sanctions, the benefit of which is enjoyed by every British subject; I also require permission to give evidence, as in other cases under the ordinary administration of the law.'

Despite Mary's star turn on the stand, when Parliament divided to vote on whether the duke was complicit in the sale of commissions, Frederick was acquitted of accepting bribes by 278 to 196. Frederick took the relatively narrow margin as a personal insult. Humiliated, furious and smarting from the fact that nearly 200 members had voted against him, he chose to resign as commander-in-chief. As his critics pointed out, this decision helpfully put a stop to any further corruption proceedings.

Unsurprisingly, the only person who came out of this scandal with anything like a jackpot was Mary. The government agreed a one-off payment for the courtesan of £10,000 and an annuity of £400, on condition that she hand over the letters she had received from the Duke of York and promise never to publish her memoirs. A born negotiator, she secured not only a larger lump sum but also an excellent education and commission for her son as part of the deal.

It was probably the easiest money Mary had ever made. Wardle, the whistle blower who had instigated proceedings against Frederick, emerged as an early winner too. He was hailed a conquering hero by the public but within months, his reputation had followed Frederick's into the gutter thanks to an upholsterer named Francis Wright. Far from being an innocent witness to proceedings, Wright claimed, Wardle had actually offered to foot the bill for Mary's expensive household furnishings if she agreed to testify against Frederick. The bill remained unpaid and when Wright appealed to Mary to settle the account, she told him to take it up with Wardle, which he was more than happy to do.

Wardle denied it all, but the courts disagreed and ordered him to pay off Wright's outstanding bill. The public were disgusted. Was there nobody who *wasn't* corrupt, they wondered.

Yet there was one more person whose name was about to enter the fray. This wasn't a politician or an upholsterer, but another prince. Those in the know about such things whispered that the person behind all the trouble was none other than Frederick's own brother, Edward, Duke of Kent. Edward served as Governor of Gibraltar in 1802 and as we shall see, his term of office was disastrous. Mary claimed that it took all of Frederick's skills to prevent Edward from being court martialled after his attempts to control the garrison collapsed into a bloody mutiny and that this had set the stage for scandal.

Though one might have expected Edward to be grateful for Frederick's apparent protection, instead Edward was furious as he had wanted a court martial to clear his name, and he swore revenge on his brother. And what better revenge could there be than snatching the position of commander-in-chief right out of Frederick's hands? When Wardle countersued Mary, she was more than happy to share this version of events with anyone who wanted to hear it. The vengeful Duke of Kent's aides had promised her £5,000 if she would agree to make Frederick's corruption public, Mary claimed, but the money had never materialised. The defence asked Wardle whether he was actually being paid by the Duke of Kent to further besmirch the reputation of Frederick by bringing about these proceedings. He denied the allegations, but the court found in Mary's favour.

And Mary, unlike some of her scandalous Georgian counterparts, knew precisely when to quit the spotlight. Though a libel suit sent her briefly to prison, she emerged as composed as ever. The consummate courtesan took her money and her notoriety and set up home in France, where she lived happily until 1852, entertaining her wide circle of friends with tales of the scandals she had known.

Wardle didn't have such a happy ending. Though the public had once rallied to pay his legal bills and even granted him the freedom of the City of London, the subsequent court cases had done immeasurable damage to his reputation. Just two years after his resignation, when the Prince of Wales became Prince Regent, Frederick was reinstated as commander-in-chief. Wardle voted against his reinstatement, but the radical Whig's career was already in its death throes. He lost his seat in 1812 and retired to a farming life, leaving the intrigues of the Commons far behind him.

Return to Office

The Duke of York was succeeded as commander-in-chief by Sir David Dundas, who had served as Frederick's deputy. At 74-years-old, Dundas brought little in the way of ambition with him and as a close friend of the duke, it was an open secret that he was nothing more than a caretaker. When the scandal had died down, went the whispers in the clubs of London, the Duke of York would once again return to his Horse Guards office.

With war still raging and Napoleon doing more than just rattling his sabre, the army needed a commander who would steer it to victory. That man was Frederick, and he was soon at the helm again. The tide that had once driven the British into retreat was on the turn and, with Wellington at its vanguard, the army was making short work of its opponents. When Napoleon was exiled to Elba, Frederick's reforms were given at least some of the credit for the army's efficiency and effectiveness. Though he recognised that the victory was really Wellington's, Frederick wrote a heartfelt letter to the Speaker of the House of Commons.

'I know not in what terms I can sufficiently express the deep sense of gratitude I feel on finding that my services in the command and administration of the British Army have once more been distinguished by the Thanks of the House of Commons.

It is to the natural energy of British soldiers, to that firm and persevering bravery which forms so distinguishing a feature in our national character, and to the pre-eminent talents of that great officer the duke [sic] of Wellington, to whom the command of our army on the Continent has been intrusted, that I must exclusively attribute the late brilliant career of his Majesty's arms.

But it is with peculiar pride I learn, that the favour of the House of Commons has induced them to ascribe to any effort of mine the smallest share in securing those splendid successes which have at once insured the future tranquillity of Europe, and crowned our exertions with unparalleled glory.'[29]

Of course, Napoleon didn't stay exiled for long and upon his escape from Elba, the British once again went into battle under the command of Wellington. The night before the fighting broke out, Wellington and his senior officers attended a glittering ball thrown by the Duchess of Richmond. Ironically, it was her husband who had nearly put a bullet through the Duke of York's curls decades earlier.

This time, the fighting was short and when the smoke cleared, Napoleon's dreams of regaining power lay in tatters. Within days, the Duke of York was doing his bit to launch a charitable campaign for casualties of the fighting but just a couple of weeks later, he was a casualty himself. Frederick fell from his horse at Oatlands and broke his arm. Happily, he recovered without incident – not always a foregone conclusion in the eighteenth century.

Passing Time

In 1816 Princess Charlotte of Wales and Prince Leopold honeymooned at Frederick's Oatlands estate. The following year, aged just 21, the only legitimate child of the Prince Regent was dead, This meant that Frederick now became second in line to the throne and, since his elder brother's health was far from ideal, it also meant that the duke stood a very good chance of one day becoming king. Yet Frederick himself had no children from his marriage to the Duchess of York. His brothers likewise had no legitimate children which, as we shall see, caused a bit of a scramble to find royal brides.

The closing years of the decade were filled with tragedy, beginning with the passing of Princess Charlotte. In 1818 Queen Charlotte died, leaving Frederick as the official guardian of his ailing father. He was believed to be a better choice to fulfil this role than his brother George, given his level head and close relationship with his father.

Just as he had been the king's favourite son during his childhood, now Frederick became his close attendant and received an annual stipend of £10,000 for his troubles. He regularly visited his father and sent updates to the royal siblings to inform them of the monarch's swiftly failing health. The seemingly robust Duke of Kent died in January 1820 after he caught a cold from his wet boots and less than six days later, George III followed him to the grave. When the Prince Regent succeeded to the throne, he too was dangerously ill, leaving Frederick poised to inherit should his elder brother pass away.

Frederick's moment never came, and the new king pulled through, but 1820 wasn't done with wringing the Duke of York out just yet.

'Never was one more truly beloved than the departed Duchess. The Duke was present at her expiring moment, and for some time previous. After the Duke had vented his distressing feeling, and had a little recovered himself, he wrote and sent off express the melancholy tidings of his loss, to the King at Windsor.'[30]

Though the Duke and Duchess of York's marriage had not been as rosy as either might have hoped, the two remained friends. Frederica Charlotte had lived a happy life at Oatlands with her menagerie of animals – which included monkeys, peacocks, two dozen dogs and more - since her arrival in England, and it was here that she died on 6 August 1820, with her husband at her side. As *The Times* observed with perhaps indecent haste just one day later, 'His Royal Highness is nearly past the age when a second marriage, though ever so carefully formed, would be likely to increase his own happiness, or to strengthen the succession in the House of Brunswick. This, however, is a subject on which it might be at present premature and indelicate to dwell.'[31]

Needless to say, there would be no second marriage for the Duke of York. Instead he honoured his late wife with a monument that was erected near her tomb at the church of St Nicholas in Weybridge. She had chosen her own resting place in an area that she loved and where she was loved in turn for her charitable and gentle nature. Her loss hit Frederick hard. George IV, however, had plans for his brother.

The Widower of York

The health of George IV had never been particularly robust and as he grew older, it became ever more lamentable. Frederick liked to tease his brother about his own position in line to the throne and after witnessing George's magnificent coronation he mused that his own inevitable crowning, when it came, would be at least as fabulous, if not more so. Yet the new king took his brother's teasing in good part, though he was all too aware that the Duke of York might still take his place.

If Frederick was to be a king, he needed a queen. George was determined to find the perfect candidate, but Frederick wasn't interested. In fact, he had already set his heart on a new – married - lady. The woman in question was Elizabeth Manners, Duchess of Rutland, with whom Frederick developed an exceptionally close, probably intimate, relationship. Frederick's ongoing financial woes were an open secret and having mortgaged Oatlands in the early nineteenth century, now he hit upon a plan to sell it and pay off his debts.

Unfortunately, like so many of the financial plans of the sons of George III, things didn't go quite as Frederick had intended. Armed with the cash from the sale and a payment of £50,000 from George IV, he went back to the racetrack and the gaming table and started gambling away the contents of his coffers. Ironically, Frederick shared his love of the turf with none other than the Duke of Rutland, husband of his intimate friend. They bonded over their mutual passions and became close confidantes.

No doubt it was the friendship with Lady Rutland rather than her husband that led Frederick into a foolhardy project that would swallow up vast reserves of his already stretched finances. He bought the buildings next to the Rutland's London home and knocked them down. On the site, he began construction on York House[32], a home suitable for a king-in-waiting. When the money dried up, Frederick kept on building and waited for a handout from the government that never came. The foundation stone was laid by the Duchess of Rutland herself. A month later she too was dead, aged just 45. At least the Dukes of Rutland and York could grieve together for the woman they had adored.

The Death of the Duke

When Queen Charlotte died in 1818 she was weakened by pneumonia and dropsy. That same illness would also touch the lives of many of her children. The Duke of York experienced the first symptoms of dropsy in 1825 and though he maintained his routine, robust and cheery as ever, his health began to decline. Still he continued as commander-in-chief and remained a familiar sight in the House of Lords, where he rose to speak out in opposition to Catholic emancipation in 1825, following his father's line on the contentious issue. His speech was a tour-de-force of passion, but his days in the spotlight were growing few.

The duke's health had begun to fail as early as 1822 when he suffered bloating and breathlessness which left him unable to sleep lying down. Whilst it had done nothing to stop him performing his duties, a relapse in 1826 was to prove far more serious. Though determined to continue serving as commander-in-chief, Frederick left London for Brighton and the supposed benefits of the sea air. Here he became so ill that in late August the Bishop of London issued the sacraments, a sure sign that things were not looking good for Frederick's recovery. Royal physicians attempted to drain a dozen pints of excess fluid from the duke's body and in doing so, they discovered that he was suffering from the early symptoms of gangrene in both legs.

Despite this Frederick soldiered on, his spirits high even though his health was weak. Upon his return to London he became a guest of the Duke of Rutland at Rutland House, but nobody was under any illusions that Frederick would recover. The Duke of York died peacefully in his armchair on the evening of 5 January 1827. His friend, Sir Herbert Taylor, recalled that the duke 'expired without any struggle or apparent pain. His countenance indeed confirmed this; it was as calm as possible, and quite free from any distortion; indeed, it almost looked as if he had died with a smile upon it. Such was the end of this amiable, kind and excellent man.'[33]

The Duke of York was still commander-in-chief at the time of his death and in public as well as the ranks, his passing was deeply mourned. Whilst George IV was savaged in his obituary, Frederick inspired poetry instead.

> 'The warrior sighs, the orphan weeps,
> For YORK, their friend and patron sleeps
> Alas! to wake no more!
>
> [...]
>
> Around the tomb, ye warriors bend
> Of ROYAL YORK, the Soldier's Friend.'

Spare a thought though for the innumerable creditors that were still unpaid once the duke's estate had been settled. Despite years of legal wrangling following his death, the Grand Old Duke never did settle his debts.

Act Four

William IV (21 August 1765–20 June 1837)

A Young Sailor

'This morning, about four o'clock, the Queen was happily delivered of a Prince. Her Royal Highness the Princess Dowager of Wales, several Lords of his Majesty's most Honourable Privy Council, and the ladies of her Majesty's Bed-chamber were present.

This great event was made known by the firing of the Tower guns. Her Majesty is, God be praised, as well as can be expected; and the young Prince is in perfect health.' [1]

William Henry was the boy who never expected to be king. Thanks to an unexpected series of events he became just that, but the road to the throne was a long and full one.

Like his brothers, much of William's childhood was spent in the royal schoolroom, where he was tutored under the watchful eye of Dr John James Majendie[2] and his aide-de-camp Jacob de Budé. As William grew, the king became ever more concerned that his son might fall under the influence of his eldest brother, the Prince of Wales. The only way to avoid this was to do just as he had done with Frederick and send William off into the world.

But he wouldn't go alone.

When William was just 12, the king visited Portsmouth to discuss with Captain Robert Digby the possibility of the young prince joining his crew. After further discussions with Rear-Admiral Samuel Hood[3], the plan was set. William would serve his country and in doing so, George hoped, escape the bad behaviour that was becoming the norm for the Prince of Wales. His berth would be the HMS *Prince George*, Digby's 89-gun flagship, and there he would be a midshipman. William wasn't impressed. He had been looking forward to painting the town red and being stuck on a ship at sea, there seemed precious little chance of that.

The king, however, had already seen worrying demonstrations of William's hot temper and quick tongue. The naval life would quell that, he was sure, and just to be certain that William would behave, he was to be accompanied by Henry Majendie, the son of his childhood tutor. Nothing was to be left to chance and the monarch issued Majendie with a set of instructions in which he laid out his expectations for William. The prince should always be kept busy and whenever he wasn't performing his naval duties, he should be concentrating on his schooling instead. From perfecting his Latin and French to saying his prayers, to ironing out 'the little tricks and rudeness, which ought to be cast off at an earlier age than He is now arrived at'[4], William had plenty to be getting on with. Just to be doubly sure that his son wouldn't shirk, the king requested that Majendie make regular reports on William's conduct to de Budé, who would monitor his progress.

On 15 June 1779, William boarded the HMS *Prince George* and began his career. Just a few weeks later, his mother wrote to him to wish him well but also, as was her way, to remind him that not only were higher powers watching, but bad influences lurked around every corner.

'You say, that You are happy & well; may You always continue to be so! By experience You will find, that, to be happy, depends very much upon Yourself [and] the most essential thing of all, is to put God always before your Eyes, & to become a sincere Christian. Believe me, no Man ever can prove a useful Member to Society, without being a good Christian. [...] If You choose this Path, You must feel Comfortable in this World, and be greatly rewarded in the next.

[...]

The Poor Duchess of Ancaster has met with another very severe stroke in the loss of her only Son, the Duke of Ancaster, who Died yesterday at seven a clock of a Putrid Fever. It is to be lamented, that this Young Man with fine Intents, a good Heart, & the Advantage of Rank, did choose to lead so idle a life, so too ruin his Health by giving himself up to Drinking, & to become Unfit to be usefull [sic] to the World, it was low Company which prevented him to shine by this Capacity; and in short it was his ruin. This is a good lesson for all Young People; Pray beware of it at all times, shun Low Company, be Humane and Charitable to Your inferiors; but do not make them Your Confidantes.'[5]

Make no mistake, the mention of the passing of the Duke of Ancaster was no mere throwaway line. It was a moral tale that Queen Charlotte intended her son to take on board. Robert Bertie, 4th Duke of Ancaster and Kesteven, was only 22 when he died and his life had been, as far as Charlotte was concerned, indolent and idle. She was utterly obsessed with protocol, piety and birth right and in mixing with the dreaded *low company*, Ancaster had sealed his fate. His death might have been caused by scarlet fever, but as far as the queen was concerned, too little prayer and too much fun played its part as well. With Wales pushing the boundaries of behaviour at home, she hoped that William's new career would turn him into a model of firm-jawed duty.

Chance would be a fine thing and there were soon reports of tantrums and angry outbursts. Before the year was out, William was writing to his father to apologise for the reports of his bad behaviour. 'I was very sorry for what I had done,' the teenaged sailor declared after a brawl, '[and] hope that I never shall be in such a temper again.'[6] Perhaps not such a surprise for this temperamental young prince.

Yet despite the fact that he was the only midshipman to travel with his very own tutor and was occasionally able to enjoy dinner aboard HMS *Victory* or dip into his annual thousand pound allowance for his support, William's life on the ocean waves wasn't a particularly privileged one. He was expected to do his share of the chores and he certainly hoped to see his share of action too. His first opportunity came at the Battle of Cape St Vincent in January 1780.

This engagement took place off the coast of Portugal, when a British fleet under the command of Admiral Sir George Rodney was escorting supply ships bound for besieged Gibraltar. Upon sighting a fleeing Spanish fleet, they gave chase and secured the surrender of the *Guipuzoana*, the sole ship-of-the-line. She was renamed the HMS *Prince William Henry* in honour of the young crewman who had been present at the rather one-sided battle and William was elated. He was given the captured ship's colours in honour of his rank, but the victory had been one that was easily won. He had yet to witness the true horrors of combat.

Just a week or so later, William realised the grim realities of battle when a brutal bombardment at sea resulted in the obliteration of a stricken vessel. To the young man it was 'a most shocking & dreadful sight. Being not certain whether it was an enemy or a friend, I felt a horror all over me.'[7] To all intents and purposes, William was still a boy when he played his part in the Battle of Cape St Vincent and though the ship was later confirmed to be a Spanish one, that knowledge alone surely wouldn't have wiped out the memory of the horror he felt as he watched the destruction of the once mighty vessel.

William arrived in Gibraltar to a hero's welcome and the king bristled with pride. Perhaps at last he might have a son who would become the dutiful young man Queen Charlotte had dreamed of when she warned William that, 'the higher the rank the more [bad behaviour] is observed.' He hoped so, anyway.

A Kidnapped Prince?

As William was sailing the ocean engaging Britain's Spanish foes, in North America the battle was raging too. Things weren't going Britain's way in the American War of Independence and when Yorktown surrendered to the forces of George Washington in October 1781, it looked as though the war was entering its endgame. Washington stood at the threshold of victory but after five long years of fighting, he needed to secure it decisively.

What could the general do that would force the hand of his opponents and bring about their capitulation?

Meanwhile, far away on a brief stopover in London, Prince William was proving that duty wasn't all that was on his mind. His life at sea had certainly made a man of him in some ways, and though he was occasionally troubled by asthma and later in life by acute attacks of gout, William was a robust and enthusiastic young fellow. Like his elder brothers, some things excited him above all others. During his return visit to England he caroused and gambled and, perhaps inevitably, fell in love. The object of his affection was a young lady named Julia Fortescue and when the king learned of his son's amorous adventures, he determined that the only thing to do was to put as much distance as possible between the couple. The prince, he decided, should go back to sea.

Little did he know it, but this was precisely the opportunity that George Washington had been looking for.

Prince William, who was then 16, arrived in New York in the winter of 1781 and was welcomed warmly by the loyalists who turned out to greet the first member of the British royal family to visit America. 'It is observable that the arrival of prince [sic] William Henry at New York, filled the British and loyalists with "joy ineffable and universal"' wrote the press. 'The very chimney sweeps smitten with the poetic flame, composed odes in his praise.'[8] He was there not on business but pleasure, revelling in being the toast of the town and receiving a procession of adoring visitors, many of whom came armed with invitations to experience the best that the city could offer, from ice skating to carousing.

There was no effort made to keep William's presence low-key and news of his escapades soon reached Washington in Morristown. He received with interest reports of the prince's love of the high life and his regular escapades through the city in search of adventure. These same reports reached George III, but William was nothing if not canny and he sent regular dispatches to his father, detailing everything he had heard whilst gadding about. He wasn't a spy as such, but he was adept at gathering information and as his son, the king knew that William could be trusted. In his letters, William described the situation in America, which he revealed was dire for the British but not all that rosy for the rebels either. Yet even as loyal New Yorkers treated the prince like a welcome superstar, Washington knew that he had been presented with an opportunity to finally achieve victory; in Prince William, he had the last piece of the puzzle.

In 1781, just before Lord Cornwallis surrendered to the rebels, Colonel Matthias Ogden began to conceive of an audacious plan to abduct the prince and demand a ransom for his release. The ransom wouldn't be payable in cash; instead, the rebels would demand freedom from British rule. Loyalist morale was crumbling all around and Ogden was confident that King George III, faced with the news of his son's abduction, would pay the ransom without a second thought. He presented the scheme to Washington, who gave it the go ahead. There was just one caveat: the prince must be treated with all due respect and care when he was in captivity.

'SIR,

The spirit of enterprise so conspicuous in your plan for surprising in their quarters, and bringing off the Prince William Henry and Admiral Digby, merits applause; and you have my authority to make the attempt in any manner, and at such a time, as your judgment may direct.

I am fully persuaded, that it is unnecessary to caution you against offering insult or indignity to the persons of the Prince or Admiral, should you be so fortunate as to capture them; but it may not be amiss to press the propriety of a proper line of conduct upon the party you command.

In case of success, you will, as soon as you get them to a place of safety, treat them with all possible respect; but you are to delay no time in conveying them to Congress, and reporting your proceedings with a copy of these orders.

Given at Morris Town, this 28th day of March 1782

G Washington

NOTE – Take care not to touch upon the ground which is agreed to be neutral – viz., from Rayway to Newark, and four miles back.'

Ogden set to work. To seize the prince from under the noses of his guards was no mean feat, but the colonel felt up to the challenge.

'It will be necessary to have four whale-boats (which can be procured without cause for suspicion); they must be well manned by their respective crews, [...] The time of embarkation must be the first wet night after we are prepared. The place is not yet agreed on, as it will be necessary to consult those skilled in the tides previous to determining, which must he put off until we are as nearly prepared as possible, for fear of inferences being drawn from our inquiries.

We most, however, set off from such part of the Jersey shore as will give us time to be in the city by half-past nine.

[…]

The Prince quarters in Hanover Square, and has two sentinels from the 40th British Regiment, that are quartered in Lord Stirling's old quarters in Broad Street, two hundred yards from the scene of action. The main guard, consisting of a captain and forty men, is posted at the City Hall – a sergeant and twelve at the head of the old slip— a sergeant and twelve opposite the coffee-house: these are troops we may be in danger from, and must be guarded against.

[…]

The order of debarkation to agree with the mode of attack, as follows: First - Two men with a guide, seconded by two others, for the purpose of seizing the sentinels; these men to be armed with naked bayonets and dressed in sailors' habits: they are not to wait for anything, but immediately execute their orders. Eight men, including guides, with myself, preceded by two men with each a crowbar and two with each an axe – these for the purpose of forcing the doors, should they be fast – and followed by four men entering the house, and seizing the young Prince, the admiral, the young noblemen, aides, etc. A captain and eighteen to follow briskly, form, and defend the house until the business is finished, and retreat a half gun-shot in our rear. A subaltern and fourteen, with half of the remaining of the boat's crew, to form on the right and left of the boats, and defend them until we return: the remainder of the crews to hold the boats in the best possible position for embarking. Necessary – two crowbars, two axes, four dark lanterns, and four large oil-clothes.

The manner of returning as follows: Six men with guns and bayonets, with those unemployed in carrying off the prisoners, to precede those engaged in that business, followed by the captain (joined by the four men from the sentry) at a half gunshot distance, who arc to halt and give a front to the enemy, until the whole are embarked in the following order: 1st, the prisoners, with those preceding them; 2nd, the guides and boatmen; 3rd, the subalterns and fourteen; 4th, the rear.'

Colonel Ogden wanted nothing left to chance and insisted that the whole matter should be carried off without raising the alarm. Washington agreed, but he remained watchful for any suggestion that the British knew of the planned abduction. He received intelligence on the number and schedule of guards employed to watch over the home of Sir Henry Clinton, the Commander-in-Chief of North America, with whom Prince William was staying, and discovered that Ogden's intelligence hadn't told the full picture. In fact, the prince's guard doubled between the hours of sunset and sunrise. A sneak attack would be all but impossible.

Colonel Ogden's plan had to be abandoned. Though Washington and the American rebels would ultimately claim the victory, they would do so without kidnapping Prince William.

When the prince prepared to leave New York in 1782, the city that had lauded and celebrated his arrival now raised an eyebrow that 'not a word is said about his departure. Many are at a loss to account for this; some suppose they were tired of the lad; others, with more probability, that they were afraid to let the time of his departure be known, lest count [sic] de Grasse[9], after the surrender of Mr. Cornwallis, should have thought him an object of his attention.'[10]

Little did they know how close to the truth they were.

In Hanover

When the American War of Independence ended in 1783, William's naval career reached a hiatus. Having settled into a life at sea with aplomb and having received the approbation of Lord Hood and Nelson alike, the young prince was disappointed to be denied any further military action. King George was more concerned that his son might have forgotten his princely ways and turned – shock, horror – into a sailor. Ironic, given William's eventual nickname of *the Sailor King*. Still the monarch was heartened by the thought that William seemed 'to wish to copy Frederick [and become an officer], but there is one very considerable difference; [Frederick], though two years older, is perfectly compliant to every advice the Officers about him give him.' With that in mind, George embarked on a plan to ensure that William's 'manners and behaviour may be formed fit for shore, and that you may in time be an Officer.'

George and Charlotte decided that their son needed to be reminded of his rank. They dispatched him to Hanover, where he was to find himself under the watchful eye of General Budé and Prince Frederick, Duke of York. He arrived in 1783, ready to embark on a rigid programme that would 'enable him to pursue his profession as an Officer, not a mere sailor.'

When Frederick and William were reunited, the elder of the two brothers would certainly have been aware of George and Admiral Lord Hood's concerns that William was far too frivolous and hot-tempered to be an officer. He wasn't so unlike the Prince of Wales in many regards, a thought that must have chilled his mother and father. Frederick was disappointed to inform them that though 'I think he is rather improved with regard to swearing, […] unluckily he had taken an idea into his head that it does not signify in what manner he behaves here, [and] he does not pay sufficient regard to any advice which General Budé gives him, and which I am convinced would be of great service to him.'[11]

William wasn't really all that interested in learning about politics or mastering the German language either. He had tasted independence and freedom and now, in his ancestral land of Hanover, he fancied tasting love too.

The young lady who took his attention was his cousin, Princess Charlotte Georgine Luise Friederike of Mecklenburg-Strelitz. She was the daughter of Queen Charlotte's brother, Charles II, Grand Duke of Mecklenburg-Strelitz, who served as governor of Hanover on behalf of George III. Charlotte was four years William's junior and when he laid eyes on her, he was smitten.

What was a boy to do? He discussed his infatuation with his brother and Budé then, torn and confused, turned to his mother for advice. Queen Charlotte was never the most effusive or affectionate woman and she was certainly not given to encouraging flirtations amongst her children. She took up her pen in October 1783 and told William in no

25. *Royalty in a Rage*, by Robert Cruikshank.

. *Design for a Regency*, by William Heath.

27. George III, by Samuel William Reynolds.

His Majesty at Cheltenham Spa, being his last Likeness draw

28. *His Majesty at Cheltenham Spa*, by Charles Rosenberg.

29. *Regency in Perspective, or, a Royal Accouchement*, by George Cruikshank.

30. Bartolomeo Pergami.

31. Queen Charlotte,
by Johann Zoffany.

WAGEMAN DEL.ᵗ   T. WOOLNOTH SCULP.ᵗ

HER MOST GRACIOUS MAJESTY
CAROLINE, QUEEN OF ENGLAND.

32. Caroline of Brunswick,
by Thomas Woolnoth.

uncertain terms that his crush on his cousin would soon pass. It wasn't the first time William fell for a girl, but it was probably the last time he asked his mother what to do about it.

'Your attachment to my Niece, which you call <u>imprudent</u> in your own letter, does not for the moment surprize [sic] me as You are of that age when Young Men are apt to fancy themselves in Love with every Sprightly Young Woman they see, or are allow'd to keep Company with. Your own good Sense, if You will make use of it, and Your Situation in Life, must shew you the impropriety of indulging a passion which cannot but prove prejudicial to all parties, <u>as there cannot be the least probability of it's [sic] ever terminating in any thing else but flirtation, which would be of essential disadvantage to the Princess who by that means might fail of being advantageously settled in life, a thing of the utmost consequence to Her, and likewise expose Your Character in a dishonourable [sic] light for pursuing & indulging an attachment which must prove fatal to the object You seem to favour. If therefore You have any real regard and Attention for Her and feel the real strength of those expressions and be possessed of any degree of Generosity & delicacy in Your Character You should try not only to conquer this unallowable passion but avoid every thing in your behaviour to Her and opportunity which can give Suspicion to the World on that Subject.</u> My Brother as well as General Budé both assure me that you have readily come into every proposal they have made to You on that Subject which I am extremely glad to hear, as I have reason to flatter myself by that means, that You will see the propriety, Necessity and Advantage of following my <u>advice</u> to the utmost, and it is upon that Hope and my Confidence in your Honour that you will put an end to this affair as speedily as possible, that I should <u>not now</u> mention it to the King, particularly as I know that My Brothers [sic] conduct in this Affair will be both friendly and prudent, and that being the case You will reflect and consider that if You <u>should pursue you will & must be the most exposed in the end.</u> I desire that you will show this letter to General Budé that He may be thoroughly acquainted with my Sentiments on this Subject and particularly as His advice may prove to You in this as upon all other occasions of infinite use to You. He has seen a great deal of the World and knows with what delicacy such an affair must be treated, and being upon the Spot himself can guide You to course and better and sooner than I am able to do now being at such a distance from You.'[12]

Ironically, Princess Charlotte would have made a suitable match for William, but his sudden infatuation hadn't given his parents time to consider other possible royal princesses who might well have been on the market. There was another reason why Charlotte hoped to keep the matter of William's affection for his cousin from her husband. The king's mental health was fragile and his spirits low. He had been battered by events in America and in the space of just 12 short months, had suffered the deaths of his two youngest sons, Prince Alfred and Prince Octavius. The death of the latter, who had been George's favourite, had hit the monarch hard and plunged him into depression which only lifted with the birth of Princess Amelia, the couple's fifteenth and last child. Queen Charlotte hoped to protect her delicate spouse from any further upset, including the impact of his son's youthful infatuations. After all, that was what the worldly-wise and trusted de Budé was expected to do.

Charlotte had one other person she hoped to prevent from hearing about William's crush: the object of it. She entreated him to 'absolutely avoid to say anything to the Princess which might create an affection in her towards you, as the consequences of that must prove fatal to her & her family, as she might be induced by that means to refuse more advantageous offers, and I hope that you are to [sic] generous to wish to be the cause of such a disappointment.'[13] Make no mistake, there was no chance that William would be allowed to marry his cousin. Queen Charlotte guessed that his sudden attraction to her was nothing but an infatuation and as time moved on and the princess was forgotten, it seemed that on this occasion the queen was right. William was soon romancing new fancies, including a young lady named Fräulein Schinbach, who would eventually go on to wed a member of the prince's travelling party, but none of these were intended to become permanent arrangements.

William wasn't looking for long-term love, even with a princess. Instead he realised that 'since I have introduced myself into the private parties of the women, I spend my time much more pleasantly than I did. I take my pleasure just like any other & go away when I please.'[14] Indeed, when he wrote to his brother the following year that he longed for 'England, England for ever, & the pretty girls of Westminster, at least to such who would not clap or pox me every time I fucked'[15], it's safe to say that his adoration for the young princess in Hanover had been long since set aside.

Though their allowances were small, William and Frederick were determined to stretch them as far as possible. Travelling under the pseudonyms of Lord Fielding and Count Hoya respectively, the brothers tasted the delights of Germany, from gambling dens to drinking houses to women. Though Budé did his best to let William make and learn from his own mistakes, he was forced to step in when an altercation around a gaming table between the prince and Baron Hardulz, who was a card sharp extraordinaire, nearly ended in a duel. Hardulz had allowed William to win big, leading the young man to believe that he was an easy opponent. His plan accomplished, once William put down his stake, Hardulz revealed his true colours and cleaned up. William was outraged and demanded a duel to restore his honour. Only now did Budé intervene, wisely convincing the nobleman to apologise to William and avoid a diplomatic incident.

In a letter to Wales, William confessed that he didn't care a jot for what people in Hanover thought of him, but he took great offence to the fact that false rumours about his conduct had reached George III, leaving the king somewhere between furious and disappointed. William, it seemed, was determined to resist all efforts to turn him into a gentleman. There was nothing for it but to send him to sea again.

Trouble at Sea

William returned from Hanover to England with the understanding that he would soon be out at sea. Whilst at home, he stopped over in Portsmouth and had just enough time to fall in love with a young lady named Sally Martin. Worry not, for he was sure to assure his brother that he did *not* debauch her. In fact, despite his enthusiasm for brothels and prostitutes, William's very specific moral code taught that 'the highest crime under Heaven next to murder is that of debauching innocent women; and it is a crime I can with a safe conscience declare I have never committed.'[16]

By this time William was at odds with the whole world. He felt sure that the king was blocking his promotion, but there was nowhere left to go if he left the navy. He briefly flirted with the idea of the army but eventually decided instead to concentrate his efforts on the branch of the forces to which he had already devoted years of his life.

During his extended sojourn at sea, William reached the rank of lieutenant and took command of his own ship, HMS *Pegasus*. Still *Coconut Head*[17], as some of the sailors called him on account of his physiognomy, remained that peculiar mixture of prince and sailor that his father had feared, given to temperamental outbursts and occasionally ungoverned passions. He sailed with Nelson in the Caribbean and the two men became close friends and colleagues, their affection fuelled by mutual respect.

Nelson was to prove an invaluable help when William got into a feud with Isaac Schomberg, an older and more experienced officer who had been personally appointed by Lord Hood to serve as first lieutenant and mentor to William. Almost as soon as Schomberg joined the crew of the *Pegasus*, the two men clashed. They had previously served together as midshipman and lieutenant but now, more than a dozen years Schomberg's junior and with far less experience, William had been promoted to captain whilst Schomberg was still his subordinate.

William loathed Schomberg and made his life as difficult as possible. He resented Hood's belief that he needed a mentor and believed that he should be trusted to command his own ship as he saw fit. He further annoyed Schomberg by refusing to dine with him whenever other captains were present, as 'we must keep officers at a distance, in order that they may remember the respect due to their captain.'[18] Eventually these petty arguments exploded over the most trivial of matters when Schomberg failed to send a boat ashore to collect hospital sheets. Under guidance from no less a man than Nelson, William arrested Schomberg and had him confined to his cabin, where Schomberg himself demanded a court martial to clear his name. However, at that point so many court martials were being issued that the navy simply didn't have the means to hear them all. Instead Schomberg was delivered safely back to Britain[19].

Yet the infamous career of Schomberg wasn't over yet. In 1787, Lord Hood appointed Schomberg to his flagship, HMS *Barfleur*, the same vessel upon which Schomberg and William first met. Prince William was outraged, perceiving this as a public humiliation, and began writing furious letters to Hood. He accused the admiral of besmirching his professional character and judgment and ended with the words, 'Much as I love and honour the Navy, […] my Lord, I shall beyond doubt resign if I have not a satisfaction from [Lord Hood].' It was an astonishing threat, but one which William ultimately didn't carry out.

William's birthday festivities weren't any less eventful for being held at sea. One of his comrades recorded the celebrations and the behaviour involved in no way reflected the sober, sombre young men that the king hoped his sons would become.

'His Royal Highness lunched with the officers in the gun-room [now the ward-room], and the interchange of condescension on the one part and of love and loyalty on the other was so often plighted in a bumper that by one o'clock scarcely one of the company could give distinct utterance to a word. By some means, I know not how (it was no easy matter), his Royal Highness contrived to crawl up to the main-deck, no doubt with the adventurous hope of being able to reach his cabin; but in an instant he was recognised by the seamen, all nearly as drunk as himself, who with unfeigned, irresistible loyalty, mounted him on their shoulders and ran with him violently from one end of the deck to the other. This was a most dangerous proceeding, for I am sure I may say that his head passed within an inch of the skids (beams) several times, and one blow at the rate they were going would inevitably have killed him.'[20]

HMS *Pegasus* arrived in Halifax, Nova Scotia, in October 1787, and William immediately set about making himself an invaluable part of the social scene. William Dyott, aide-de-camp to George III, describes in his diaries a young man filled with confidence who had a weakness for women and no qualms about showing it.

'He would go into any house where he saw a pretty girl, and was perfectly acquainted with every house of a certain description in the town,'[21] wrote Dyott, a fact understandably omitted from the reports that William himself sent home to his father.

As winter drew in, the fleet headed home. The journey was dangerous and costly, but *Pegasus* survived to reach port in December 1787. William was glad to be in Plymouth and in the arms of a merchant's daughter named Sally Winne, but Christmas with the family and the inevitable 'Christmas box or New year's gift [of] a family lecture for immorality, vice, dissipation and expence [sic]'[22] was looming. Yet Sally Winne, just like her predecessors, was a temporary arrangement and in 1788 William was in Halifax, Nova Scotia, aboard the *Andromeda*. So inflamed was his passion for Sally that the king determined this was the only way to keep them apart, but he little suspected what would happen upon his son's arrival in Canada.

Back on dry land, William raised the roof, drinking and debauching at every opportunity. Dyott described a man who, when he trusted someone, was the best friend you could hope for, but was easily offended and knew how to bear a grudge. William could be glittering company and he hosted magnificent balls and sumptuous dinners on board his ship to which the great and the good were invited. It was during this stopover that William fathered the first of what would be many illegitimate children. His son, William Henry Courtney, would go on to have a naval career of his own. It was never revealed who his mother had been.

This was not what the king had envisioned when he dispatched his boy over the Atlantic to keep him from the arms of Sally Winne. In fact, the plan had gone spectacularly wrong and with George III's mental health in crisis, it was left for the Prince of Wales to summon his younger brother home once more. William's naval career was over.

The Marriage That Wasn't

When William reached England, he discovered that the threatened catastrophe had passed, and his father was recovering. With nothing else to occupy his time, William decided that the time had come for him to be a duke, a rank which the Prince of Wales had begun moves to secure for him. Frederick was already a duke, William noted, and he believed that to deny him the same honour was an unforgiveable oversight as well as clear evidence of favouritism. Previously, the Prince of Wales had encountered the resistance of William Pitt when it came to giving a dukedom to William, and the king was no keener to see it done, believing his third son had not yet earned such a distinction. However, William had an ace up his sleeve. He simply declared that if he couldn't serve his country in the Lords, he would do so in the Commons instead and threatened to stand for Parliament in the constituency of Totnes. Faced with this potential new source of embarrassment, the king acquiesced.

In 1789 George III agreed that William would henceforth be known as Duke of Clarence and St Andrews and Earl of Munster. As he signed the papers, the Tory sovereign bitterly commented that, 'I well know that it is another vote added to the Opposition,'[23] and well he might, for his Whig sons were his natural political foes. From now on, William would be entitled to an allowance of £12,000 per year and apartments in St James's Palace. With his title secured, William made his presence felt in the House of Lords, speaking on a variety of issues.

He became a familiar sight in Westminster, where he liked to make his voice heard, sometimes to the embarrassment of his family. When he spoke at the debate on a proposed Adultery Bill in 1800, William furiously branded those who committed adultery as 'an insidious and designing villain, who would ever be held in disgrace and abhorrence by an enlightened and civilised society', completely ignoring the fact that his own brothers were well known for their enthusiastic embracing of all things adulterous. Though this was certainly eccentric, his views on slavery were unswerving and concrete. William was very much a product of his class and would have known many slave owners; as such, he opposed abolition with every fibre of his being and argued that taking people from their homelands to sell them into a life of grinding labour was actually a blessing. Even in the eighteenth century his opinions shocked some members of the Lords and the public, but there were plenty of people who were happy to agree with him.

On the matter of slavery, as on so many others, William was given to rambling speeches that left many of his fellow peers confused. He argued that the key to saving the slave trade was to ensure that slaves were 'immersed in illiterate stupidity' rather than educated and that 'the trade and the slavery must stand together.' In his opinion, slave owners were decent people and slaves were on the whole happy, declared the prince. Anyone who disagreed with him – and in this he included the celebrated and dedicated abolitionist, William Wilberforce – was either a fanatic or a hypocrite.

The speech resulted in furious scenes in the House of Lords. The prince was censured for his language and he was held up to ridicule and outrage. We would rightly expect no other outcome than this, but William was both surprised and unflappable. He was sure that he was right, and nothing would change his mind.

Yet even as he was causing a rumpus in the Lords, some outlandish rumours claimed that William didn't remain in London at all. In 1880 a scandalous book was published in Germany that purported to contain clandestine letters between the by-then-late King William IV and a young lady named Caroline von Linsingen, supposedly his secret wife. The press, by now four decades into the reign of Queen Victoria, fell over themselves to pour delighted and rather scandalised praise on it.

The story has all the marks of Gothic fiction, from a forbidden love to a broken heart and even a brush with premature burial, yet what were the facts in the romance of William IV and Caroline von Linsingen?

Before we unpick *that*, let's find out the supposed truth.

Caroline was born in 1768. She was the daughter of Lieutenant General Wilhelm von Linsingen, a man so trusted by the House of Mecklenburg-Strelitz that he was chosen to accompany Queen Charlotte when she set out for England to marry George III. He remained a trusted and loyal retainer and it was through him that William and Caroline supposedly met when the prince visited Hanover in 1790. They danced at a ball and it was love at first sight, but Queen Charlotte forbade any suggestion of marriage, no matter how much her son begged. Still their romance blossomed and a year later, it carried them to the altar at Pyrmont.

Grab a tissue, because the letter below was supposedly written by the blushing bride herself. We'll discover whether there was any truth in it a little later.

'BLANSKO, 21st August

4am

Once more has the day come round for me, on which I became the happiest of mortals. Once more I am to feel the blissful joy which lay in the certainty of being wholly his: once more, too, all a martyr's anguish is mine, that I am severed from him, for ever, for this life! How I tremble, how my heart throbs, how all the past revives!

I hear my brother's voice, urging them to saddle the horses without delay. The maid enters with the breakfast; [Caroline's brother] Ernst is behind her; both marvel that I am ready dressed; my brother entreats me to be calm. Now, as I hear the tramp of horses to bear me to his arms, I tremble just as I did then; "I come, I come," I cry, yet I remain rooted to the spot. Ernst bends to kiss me, but I withdraw my lips, for even a brother's kiss seems to me a theft from William at this holy time. He understands me, and smiles.

And now I hurry down the staircase. [A servant] is holding my horse. […]

Scarcely am I seated before I am in full gallop along the familiar road; and in a short half-hour I sink into William's arms; in silence he clasps me to his bosom, leading me into a peasant's hut. […] He shows me the clothes that had been sent on before for me, kneels before me for a few minutes, then leaves me, but no sound escapes our lips. What earthly blessedness can match this godlike rapture!

I hurriedly dress myself. I was forced to leave to William the choice of my apparel. A robe of dazzling whiteness, a broad gold belt with diamond clasp, this formed my whole bridal adornment. William now returns. He rushes to my arms, but what we then said to each other no tongue, no pen may ever repeat. With words such as these seraphs might greet one another! Ernst enters; he has a wreath of fresh myrtle in his hand.

[…]

[Ernst] pressed the wreath upon my brow, moistened as it was by his and William's tears. And now they both raised me up (for I was kneeling before Ernst), and I lay for a few seconds in their arms. My brother signalled William to withdraw.

[At the chapel] we knelt down before the minister. William's responses were uttered in a clear and solemn tone, yet he trembled no less violently than myself. Indescribable were my feelings as, in the grey haze of morning, (it was between five and six o'clock,) I gave myself up wholly to my beloved. Was it the sacred ceremony that kept me from perishing from my mingled anguish and bliss? All onlookers wept with emotion. We rose, and now, as in this peaceful house of God William took me to his arms as wife, pressing his picture to my breast, reiterating his vows of eternal love.

[Later] he stayed with me alone for a quarter of an hour. Taking off the sash and wreath, he put on my hat for me, and then went half reverentially to the door. At this juncture he seemed a very god: all that which in this blessed time he said to me bore such thorough witness to his great, his noble, kingly heart, that I marvelled at the good fortune which suffered me to call this, ay this man, my own. I rushed after him, and, falling at his feet, kissed the hand he had given me at the altar. He quickly raised me. " I only, beloved wife," said he, "may kneel to you; that is my place: calm, calm yourself. We must needs be so to-day. Whether or no Fate's chill shadow fall on us, our bond of union is eternal – you are mine; and I, I am Caroline's blissful husband!"[24]

And should there be any doubt that the marriage was consummated in the eyes of God and the law, Caroline was quick to clear that up too.

'We had no intrusion to fear, and we passed two hours of heavenly bliss together – the first happy ones of a most happy married life: they were to be followed by many such. Oh! how safe, how blessedly calm I felt as I lay in the arms of this noble man! We could never have believed it; yet so it was, our love, our mutual trust, had gained as it were in fervour and intensity. A gentle gloom surrounded us; there was only the shaded light of a single taper burning on a table. He said to me that already yesterday Ernst had promised this hour to him, to compensate for the sacrifices of the daytime, which otherwise he would not have had strength enough to have made.'[25]

But of course, the fate of our lovers was to be an unhappy one. When Caroline's father found out about the marriage, he was furious, even though William did his best to convince his bride's parents that he would forever love and care for their daughter. Ultimately it was not to be, and *Coconut Head* was parted from the arms of his secret wife forever and forced into a divorce, leaving them both heartbroken.

But fate hadn't finished with Caroline. In 1792, she grew frail and emaciated, ravaged by fever and spasms that her doctors could do nothing to fight. Eventually her body took one last wretched breath and she grew still. The doctors pronounced their unhappy patient dead and left her to her attendants, who dressed the stiffening corpse in her finest clothes and surrounded her with flowers. Yet there was one among the eminent physicians who wasn't happy with the final diagnosis.

The young and rather dashing Dr Adolph Meineke returned to Caroline's bedside and discovered that she was not dead, but in a somnambulistic sleep. Like Sleeping Beauty, he revived her and the two were married, though Caroline's heart forever belonged to the Sailor King. In his last letter to his lost bride, the man who once longed for a girl who wouldn't pox him when they fucked wrote, 'In the intoxication of our mutual passion we often felt that we had but one heart, one soul, that we were but one being, down to the veriest trifles; and is it possible that this should have an end?'[26]. In fact, it was very possible indeed, because that tragic, tortured love story was naught but a fiction from beginning to end.

Although the Royal Marriages Act would have rendered a marriage between William and Caroline invalid, the entire love story explodes the very second we consider the fact that William was nowhere near Germany in 1790, but safely ensconced in London. Unless the prince was able to split himself in two, the secret marriage to Caroline must be nothing but a fairy tale.[27]

William's early biographer Robert Huish, however, does provide an explanation for what was to be an enduring Victorian legend. He discovered that there was indeed a lady in Hanover with whom William had a liaison and who, it appears, may have provided him with at least one illegitimate child. When she arrived in London with personal and intimate papers that proved her connection to the prince, he was left with no choice but to make financial arrangements with her. Perhaps this was the genesis of the strange story of Caroline and the prince.

Mrs Jordan

Dorothea Jordan's life was the Georgian era in a microcosm. From rags to riches and back again, via a change of identity, a litany of lovers and two decades at the side of a prince.

Dorothea was born to an Irish father and Welsh mother in 1761 and she was raised in Dublin. Young Dora, as she was known, was illegitimate. Though her mother, Grace, styled herself *Mrs Bland*, wife of Francis, the couple had in fact been married only for the briefest of periods. Bland was underage and once his father learned of the wedding, he had it annulled and cut the young couple off without a penny. Together Grace and Francis were sure they could make a go of it in the world of theatre, with Grace treading the boards and Francis working as a stagehand, but it wasn't to be. Francis Bland wasn't content with his little family and as the years passed, he became consumed with animosity towards his parents, who enjoyed comfortable lives whilst he was forced to work his fingers to the bone.

When Dora was 13, Bland joined the military and abandoned his family to chase his fortune. Back home in Ireland, times were harder than ever for the family he left behind. Young Dora took a job working as a milliner's assistant, ploughing every penny she made back into the family's empty coffers whilst for Francis, things were on the up. He married a wealthy woman named Catherine Mahony and remained at her side until his death in 1778. There was no inheritance for Dora and her family from her deceased father.

Desperate for money and by now impoverished, the Bland family needed a stroke of good fortune. As no stranger to the stage, Grace Bland decided that her daughter was far too charming to be a milliner's apprentice when there was more money to be made in the theatre. It was time for a career change.

The young Dora made her Dublin debut when she was just 18, appearing in Henry Fielding's *The Virgin Unmasked*. It was the start of what was to become a notorious and illustrious career. Though Grace believed that her daughter's beauty and charm would be the key to her success, it wasn't only her face and talent that kept audiences flocking in over the years. True she had innate comic timing and an attractive singing voice, but what the punters really loved was her legs. Dora was soon specialising in so-called *breeches* roles, where she played young male leads. One flash of her calves sent the audience wild. Dora had hit on a winning formula.

'In Mrs Jordan were combined all the qualities requisite to the formation of a comic actress in the sprightly, joyous, romping style, with full power to embody genuine feeling, and send a warm of generous sentiment home to the heart. Her face, if not exactly beautiful, was irresistibly agreeable; her person and gait elegant and elastic; her voice, in singing, perfectly sweet and melodious, and, in speaking, clear and impressive; her enunciation, whether she spoke or sung, always gave full effect to words she had to deliver; her pronunciation was peculiarly elegant and correct; and she retained some accents of her native Ireland, which, far from impairing, enhanced the richness of her tones, and the simplicity of her expressions'[28]

With Dora's new success came stage door Johnnies and if Grace was shepherding her daughter's career with aplomb, she was rather less successful when it came to men. Dora's first proposal came from Lieutenant Charles Doyne, a soldier of reasonable but not exceptional wealth and prospects. Grace told her daughter to reject his suit because she was bound for greater things. She was determined that Dora wouldn't surrender her rising star for the sake of a lovesick suitor. Besides, what help would a husband be to an actor with the whole world at her feet? No, if Dora was going to have a gentleman, Grace was going to make sure that it would be for professional as well as personal benefit. There must be someone out there who combined influence with romance, surely?

That someone was Richard Daly, the married manager of Cork's Theatre Royal, and a man who never said *no* to a good-looking prospect.

This dandified, squinting impresario had managed to survive no less than sixteen duels in just two years, and he was used to landing on his perfectly shod feet. When Grace fell ill, Daly loaned Dora the money she needed to pay for her mother's medical treatment but when the time came to collect on the debt, it was with added and intimate interest. Dora became the theatre manager's lover and fell pregnant by him at the age of 20. What an irony it must've been for Grace to see off Dora's suitor for fear of the damage to her career, only to find herself with a pregnant and distinctly unmarried leading lady on her hands. Not only that, but they still owed Daly the money he had loaned them for Grace's medical treatment and Dora would have to take at least *some* time away from the stage when the baby came along.

There was only one thing for it: Dora had to be spirited away from her creditor as soon as possible. They needed to put some distance between them and where better for an aspiring star with a clutch of excellent reviews beneath her expanding-belt than England? Dora and her mother fled, leaving their unpaid debts and Daly far behind.

The road eventually brought them to Leeds and Tate Wilkinson's well-respected theatre company. It was here that Dora Bland became Dora Jordan, the name under which she was to become a star. That was Wilkinson's doing too, as he explained to an acquaintance who questioned him on Mrs Jordan's unexpected change of identify.

'As I had never heard that Miss Bland was married, I afterwards enquired of Wilkinson the cause, and he replied, "her name? – why, God bless you, my boy! I gave her that name, – I was her sponsor.'
'You!' –
'Yes: when she thought of going to London, she thought Miss sounded insignificant, so she asked me to advise her a name. – Why, said I, my dear, you *have crossed the water, so I'll call you Jordan*; and, by the memory of Sam! if [sic] she didn't take my joke in earnest, and called herself Mrs. Jordan ever since.'[29]

Tate Wilkinson was an incorrigible teller-of-tales, so how much truth there is in his version of events is debateable. There was certainly no wedding to a *Mr* Jordan, however, and the symbolism of Dora's escape from Daly across the Irish Sea, much as the persecuted Israelites crossed the River Jordan to sanctuary, certainly has an element of the theatrical about it. Whatever the truth, the name stuck. Dora was to be known, both with respect and mockery, as *the Jordan*[30] for the rest of her days.

Once she had reached England and given birth to Richard Daly's daughter[31], Dora's career really took off. Her stage-door admirers clamoured for her attentions and to secure them, they were happy to settle Dora's outstanding debts to Daly. She enjoyed a passionate relationship with George Inchbald, her leading man in Wilkinson's theatre company, but the longed-for marriage proposal never materialised. Eventually Dora decided that the time had come to move on, both personally and professionally. Once she had conquered the north, Dora moved to London and there she lit up the comedic stage, charming suitors and audiences alike. It was here, in 1786, that she met Richard Ford.

Ford was a lawyer and magistrate and Dora fell for him hard. She honestly believed that this ambitious, respectable man would make an honest woman of her, but he never had any intention of doing so. Despite or perhaps because of this, Dora took his surname as her own and for half a decade the pair lived as husband and wife. Together they had three children, two of whom lived to adulthood.[32] Just as she had with Inchbald, Dora waited for her lover to make his move and propose and just like Inchbald, he did no such thing. She was still waiting for the proposal in 1790 when she performed at the Theatre Royal, Drury Lane, in the role that would give her another of her nicknames.

The role was that of Little Pickle in *The Spoil'd Child* and Dora played the mischievous, cheeky little boy to perfection. So well-received was she that the play became one of the hottest tickets in London and among those who snapped up a seat was the Duke of Clarence, as William was now known. He must have liked what he saw because he became a dedicated follower of Dora and the gossip columnists were swift to pick up on the fact. When a newspaper reported that a certain illustrious gentleman could be relied upon to be in Dora's audience, it was to be the start of an enduring and lengthy affair.

'The Jordan is at length in tow of the royal sailor. A shot of a life-annuity of 1000l. and the refusal of her late Commander Ford, To marry, brought this prime dramatic sailor to.'[33]

Just as his brother had been enchanted by Mary Robinson, William was soon besotted with Dora and the press lapped it up. Though Ford had fathered two of her three surviving children, he and Dora were not actually husband and wife so once the Duke of Clarence showed an interest, Dora was ready to move on. By autumn 'the dramatic JORDAN has lately proved too DEEP to BE FORDED!'[34], and that six-year affair was over. Today we're used to seeing the dirty linen of the rich and famous washed in public on a constant basis and the Georgians were no different. Their appetite for scandal was unmatched and when the whirlpool dragged in an actress and a royal prince, what could be better for the box office or circulation figures?

When Dora left Ford's house, she didn't take her children with her. Instead she sent them to live with her sister in Brompton and arranged to pay for their care. The press and public, however, interpreted this move as a neglectful one. Dora was cancelling engagements left, right and centre due to ill health and the more she cancelled, the more agitated her audience became. To them, the cancellations came at a suspiciously convenient time and seemed to line up precisely with the start of her relationship with William. When she rehomed her children, it was all the proof they needed that Mrs Jordan was putting personal pleasure ahead of career and family. So fevered did speculation become that Richard Ford eventually wrote a letter to a friend that was intended to silence his ex-lover's critics once and for all. Somehow – who can *imagine* how – the letter was leaked to the newspapers and shared with the lady's prosecutors.

'Lest any insinuations should be circulated to the prejudice of Mrs. JORDAN, in respect to her having behaved improperly towards her children in regard to pecuniary matters, I hereby declare that her conduct has in that particular been as laudable, generous, and as like a fond mother, as in her present situation it was possible to be. – She has indeed given up for their use every sixpence she has been able to save from her theatrical profits; she has also engaged herself to allow them 55l. per annum; and at the same time settled 50l. a year upon her sister. It is but bare justice to her, for me to assert this, as the father of those children.

[...]

In gratitude for the care Mrs. JORDAN has ever bestowed upon my children, it is my consent and wish that she should, whenever she pleases, see and be with them, provided her visits are not attended by any circumstances which may be improper to them, or unpleasant to me.'[35]

Dora and the duke were a couple at last and the newspapers went wild to report on their every move. Some were mischievous, suggesting that 'Mrs. JORDAN and the DUKE of CLARENCE were cheek by jowl in their box on Monday – the latter seemed more than usually attentive'[36], whilst others were downright obscene. Can you imagine even the most salacious modern tabloid wryly commenting that the Duke of Clarence's favourite song was, *On the Banks of the Jordan We'll Merrily Play*, without incurring the wrath of the royal PR machine?

Yet though gossip might be entertaining and kept the Georgian fourth estate in cash and scandal, it was no substitute for seeing Dora Jordan on stage, doing what she did best. But the cancellations continued and for even the most loyal fan, there was a breaking point. Whilst Dora was spotted out and about with William regularly enough, when the time came to put in a few hours work, all too often, she was nowhere to be seen. Little Pickle was claiming exhaustion, but she didn't seem too exhausted to move to a pricy new neighbourhood and take regular outings in one of the city's grandest and showiest coaches. Like plenty of other illustrious and flamboyant Georgians, Dora didn't believe in hiding her wealth.

In the playhouses where her disappointed audiences waited, meanwhile, there was a bit of a revolution taking place. Dora had burned too many bridges with her late-notice cancellations – sometimes not sending word until the curtain was almost ready to rise – and managers and patrons alike were tired of it. Dora was making a name for herself as unreliable, and that meant that more than ever she might end up beholden to the duke for the upkeep of her opulent lifestyle. Fine in theory, but William was hardly the most reliable man to have his hands on the purse strings.

'The Haymarket Manager certainly does all in his power, to accommodate the abilities of his Company to the entertainment of the public. – But he cannot be answerable for the whim or caprice of any individual Performer –

The audience of Saturday took the business up in this point of view – but they rejected the *Farce of High Life Below Stairs*, because they paid their money to see *Richard Couer de Lion* – and as to Mrs. *Jordan's* indisposition, they considered that not to be an obstacle, while Mrs. Crouch, who originally performed the part, was in the House! They carried their point, and Mrs. Crouch rose to higher esteem than ever, by considerably lessening the consequence of Mrs. Jordan.

If Mrs. Jordan really was ill she is to be pitied, because she certainly has lost much in public estimation by her conduct of Saturday: for the apology was not considered by the audience to originate in truth, as it was not sent to the Prompter until after the doors were opened.

Another matter in further proof of this Lady not being in favour with the public was, that when one part of the House called out for the Manager, another part lustily bawled out "No Manager" – "send *Clarence* forth."[37]

For Dora and William, of course, the Royal Marriages Act meant that there was no chance of them making their union official. Despite this, there was no doubting their commitment and William marked it by giving Dora a diamond and gold ring. In fact, at the time of William's supposed heart-breaking divorce from Caroline von Linsingen on German soil, he was busy setting up home with Dora Jordan. Over the years that followed they would welcome no less than ten children[38]. All of them bore the surname *FitzClarence.*[39]

The New Century

Settled with Dora, William seemed to have finally found some measure of domestic harmony but in other ways, little had changed. William still couldn't balance his budget and his eye watering debts were spiralling out of control. By 1795 he owed his creditors in excess of £50,000 and even the sale of property he had purchased in Richmond couldn't put much of a dent in his debt. Still he pressed on, scraping by on handouts from his father and Parliament where he could, and quietly climbing the naval ranks despite not spending any further time on active service. In fact, when Britain went to war with France in 1793, William was so keen to serve that he wrote to the Lords of the Admiralty to beg them for the chance.

'If the rank which I hold in the navy operates as an impediment to my obtaining command of a ship without that squadron being attached to it, I will willingly relinquish that rank under which I had formerly the command of a ship, and serve as a volunteer on board any ship to which it may please your lordships to appoint me. All I require is active service, and that when my gallant countrymen are fighting the cause of their country and their sovereign, I may not have the imputation thrown upon me of living a life of inglorious ease, when I ought to be in front of danger.'

It was not to be and even letters to the king and Nelson made no difference. William had made a controversial speech in Parliament, opposing the war between Britain and France, and he believed this had ultimately thwarted his naval career. Denied the opportunity to see the front line and dissatisfied with the government's handling of the war, William made loud and repeated criticisms of it at every opportunity, confirming the view that he was entirely unfit for senior governmental office. So offended were the likes of Pitt by his unbridled criticisms that the king eventually stepped in and asked his son to refrain from any further criticisms. 'I have promised to be quiet,' he dryly sighed in reply.

Perhaps to mollify William, he was promoted to Vice Admiral and then, in 1798, to Admiral. These were nominal promotions at best, and William knew it.

By this time, William and Dora were living at Bushy Park, a royal estate, where William was the ranger, and their spending was continuing unabated. Once the young rake who had raised hell, now he was settling happily into the life of a family man and doting father, entirely at odds with the public image of Wales, who pinged from woman to woman like a pinball. Though it might seem odd that George and Charlotte were prepared to countenance this long, public and rather fecund affair, and certainly knew their illegitimate grandchildren, it shouldn't. William had made no embarrassing move to marry Dora and as the third son, the chances of him ever succeeding to the throne were remote at best, so there was little need for him to worry about the matter of heirs and spares. In fact, Lord Liverpool even commented that things between William and his father were so settled 'that the King jokes with him about Mrs Jordan', something that would have been unthinkable for the Prince of Wales and his paramour.

Yet all that was set to change.

For twenty years Dora and William had lived in domestic harmony, unmarried but very much a couple, both in public and private. William frequented the House of Lords and Dora played the duchess at home, firmly ensconced at the head of a household that relied heavily on her earnings. Though in the country at large things had certainly changed, with the king's irreversible slide into dementia and the establishment of the Regency, at Bushy Park all had stayed the same for years. That well-oiled and smooth pattern of life lurched to a shuddering halt when the Prince Regent assumed power. Though the royal sons were many, their legitimate heirs were few. The Prince Regent himself could boast only one child, Princess Charlotte of Wales, and with his marriage having ended in mutual loathing, there were unlikely to be any more. The Duke of York had no heirs and even William, with his houseful of children, could claim no actual legitimate offspring who could take their place in the line of succession. A chill wind was blowing, and it would carry William to the altar and Dora to catastrophe.

In 1811 William finally took the decision to end his relationship with Dora once and for all. Suddenly possessed by the need to do his duty and take a legal wife who might give him an heir, as the year came to an end, he had a deed of separation drawn up. Dora, who had worked throughout their relationship in order to finance her lover's lavish tastes, was summoned from her theatrical engagement in Cheltenham to meet William. He presented her with the document that officially ended their affair and soon afterwards, it became public knowledge. Whereas she had been the object of derision for neglecting her audiences, now both barrels were turned on the Duke of Clarence.

As Dora played the northern circuit to ever dwindling audiences, poetry and caricature mocking William began to seep onto the market.

Dora had her own suspicions as to what had caused the break between her and her lover and she believed, quite rightly, that it came down to the matter of cash. What she perhaps didn't know was that William already had his eye on her replacement and fancied two women as the ideal candidates. The first was Margaret Mercer Elphinstone, a close friend of his niece, Princess Charlotte of Wales. She rejected the duke without a second thought[40], so he turned his attention to an even greater prospect and a woman to whom money was no object.

Catherine Tylney-Long was a friend of William's daughters and she also happened to be worth a fortune. In fact, Miss Tylney-Long was known as the richest commoner in the country thanks to a vast inheritance she received at the age of 16. Sadly, that inheritance made her the target of every fortune hunter in the United Kingdom and nobody loved a fortune more than the royal princes.

William, by now appointed to the position of Admiral of the Fleet, was determined to marry Catherine but he lost her hand to the Duke of Wellington's nephew, William Wellesley-Pole[41]. 'As soon as it was known by Mrs. JORDAN, that the Duke of CLARENCE was in pursuit of another Lady,' said the press, raking over the bones of the affair, 'the die was cast for their separation.'[42]

The couple's children were heartbroken that their happy home should be torn apart by ambition, but Dora remained loyal to the man who had cast her off. Still, she knew full well what had motivated him to leave her.

> 'My mind is beginning to feel somewhat reconciled to the *shock and surprise* it has lately received, for could *you* or the *world* believe that we never had, for twenty years, the *semblance* of a QUARREL. But this is so well known in our domestic circle, that the astonishment is the *greater*! MONEY, money, my good friend, or the *want* of it, has, I am convinced, *made* HIM, at this moment, the *most wretched* of MEN; but having done *wrong*, he does not like to retract. But with all his excellent qualities, his domestic virtues, his love for his *lovely* children, what must he not at this moment *suffer*! His distresses should have been relieved *before*; but this is *entre nous*.
>
> All his letters are full of the most unqualified praise of my conduct; and it is the most heartfelt blessing to know that, to the

best of my power, I have endeavoured to deserve it. I have received the greatest kindness and attention from the R[egent], and every branch of the Royal Family, who, in the most *unreserved terms*, deplore this melancholy business.

[I will] not hear the D. of C. unfairly abused; he has done *wrong*, and he is *suffering* for it; but, as far as he has left it in his *own power*, he is doing every thing KIND and NOBLE, even to the *distressing* HIMSELF.'[43]

As part of their formal separation, William made Dora an offer of £1,500 a year, plus a further allowance of £1,500 for their daughters, who would remain with their mother. He was set on the military life for his sons, whether in the navy or army. All his sons other than Augustus followed his wishes, whilst the latter joined the clergy and later became William's Chaplain in Ordinary. None of Dora's sons saw her regularly after the split. Her eldest daughter, Sophia, was William's favourite child and she longed to be with her father rather than her mother. William, however, told her that it was quite impossible. She would live with her mother, whilst the boys would stay with him.

'I never wish either to say or write an angry word to you: but I cannot approve of your now wishing to live with me: I must be the best judge and am your best friend: [...] the boys <u>must</u> live with me and will occasionally visit their mother: till every thing is settled between me and your mother there is not any hurry about her taking a house unless a very cheap and convenient one offers.'[44]

Dora's allowances were largely dependent on a clause in the agreement that stated she would lose the custody of her daughters and forfeit the £1,500 intended to pay for their care if she ever returned to the stage. The heartbroken Dora agreed to the terms but the allowance she had been given was simply not enough to meet her lavish living costs. When her financial struggles became public knowledge and William was blamed for her troubles, Dora even wrote an open letter to the press begging them to go easy on her ex-partner. It was the polar opposite of a kiss and tell hatchet job, and even more remarkable for being so.

'In the love of truth, and in justice to his Royal Highness, I think
it is my duty thus publicly and unequivocally to declare, that his
liberality to me has been noble and generous in the HIGHEST
DEGREE.'[45]

William, meanwhile, continued to count every penny and went cap in
hand to whoever would spare a coin or two. He escaped the United
Kingdom to undertake a tour of the low countries and a round of troop
inspections across German territories and by the time he returned to
Bushy House Dora and the children were long gone. Curiously, now she
was no longer his partner, William set about decorating the home they
had shared for so long with portraits of Dora. Too little, too late.

Ultimately, Dora's return to the stage was inevitable and when she took
theatrical work to help pay off some debts that her children had incurred,
William was as good as his word. Both the custody of the girls and the
majority of Dora's allowance were removed, marking the start of her final
slide into penury. Before Dora threw in her lot with William, she had
been financially independent and, as a star of the stage, had lived the sort
of A-list lifestyle you might expect. Yet during the twenty years she spent
with the Duke of Clarence, her earnings had become less and less whilst
his spending skyrocketed. Now they were apart, and it was she who was
left trying to settle their debts, loyal to her prince to the last.

'We are sorry to state that this charming Actress is no more. The
Paris papers received on Tuesday state that she lingered in a state
of insensibility till Friday the 5th inst. When she expired at two
o'clock in the morning, at her apartments in St. Cloud.'[46]

Dora Jordan died in 1816 in France, having been forced out of England
and into a life of poverty to escape her creditors. Years later, William
commissioned a statue of Dora and two of their children from the sculptor,
Francis Chantrey. He wept as he told Chantrey what he wanted, no doubt
reflecting on all that he had surrendered in the pursuit of money.

Marrying Adelaide

With Dora lost to him, William redoubled his efforts to find a rich wife and in 1817, it became more important than ever that he did so. George III was completely incapacitated and with the health of the high-living and ever-expanding Prince Regent questionable at best, there needed to be someone ready to step into the breach. When the heiress to the throne, Princess Charlotte of Wales, died within hours of giving birth to a stillborn baby, the line of succession began to look shakier than ever[47].

The time had come for William to marry and start turning out the heirs and spares that his brothers had failed to produce. For a time, he fixed his ambitions on a Danish princess who turned him down flat, then on Miss Wykeham, a vastly rich and eccentric Brighton heiress who wore spurs and leapt five-barred gates. William had all the chat and told her that 'he had not a single farthing, but if she would like to be a Duchess, and perhaps a Queen, he would be happy to arrange it.'[48] The queen and his brothers, however, would have none of it and William withdrew. Yet with no British heiress exactly desperate to take him on, where was William to find a likely bride?

William charged his brother, Adolphus, Duke of Cambridge, with finding him the perfect wife. Adolphus duly took off for Europe and a tour of the German courts, where he was sure they would find an ideal candidate. The first to fit the bill was 20-year-old Augusta of Hesse-Kassel but her father wasn't entirely sold on her being married off to William, whose debts and disastrous love life were well known to him. This suited Augustus, who became betrothed to her himself instead.

William's next preferred candidate was Adelaide of Saxe-Meiningen. Born in 1792, she was the daughter of Luise Eleonore of Hohenlohe-Langenburg and George I, Duke of Saxe-Meiningen, and she appeared to have all the attributes necessary to make an excellent Duchess of Clarence. She was young, highly religious and entirely untouched by scandal. Even better, she would bring with her a handsome dowry of 20,000 florins. Not only that, but she was more than happy to accept William's illegitimate children without complaint and William knew that, once he had the ring on her finger, he could look forward to some rather generous parliamentary allowances.

In fact, he was wrong on the latter count. Parliament examined William's debts and declared that, whilst it would settle some of them, it would not grant him an allowance any greater than £6,000 per year. Instead, said the House, the royal family should provide for its children just as any other family was expected to. William was outraged and declared that in that case, he wouldn't get married at all. This caused an uproar and though William eventually reconsidered and agreed to the marriage, he remained piqued at the decision not to grant him a fat annuity in return. At least he could count on that dowry.

Adelaide's parents were more than happy to accept the hand of a British prince for their daughter and in the summer of 1818, she and her mother travelled to London accompanied by a large retinue and a coach that was filled to the brim with luggage. Here she was received by William and the Prince Regent at Grillon's Hotel on Albemarle Street and after a successful meeting, the wedding date was set for one week later. William had no illusions about the marriage and wrote to his eldest son, George, to tell him that, '[Adelaide] is doomed, poor, dear, innocent young creature, to be my wife. I cannot, I will not, I must not ill use her.' And to his credit, he kept his word. Perhaps surprisingly, the Duke of Clarence was faithful to the end of his days.

Due to the parlous state of Queen Charlotte's health, the wedding was to be held in her drawing room at Kew, to ensure that she would be able to attend. As pious and domestic as ever, Charlotte no doubt would have approved wholeheartedly of the unassuming and limelight-shunning young Adelaide after twenty years of Dora Jordan. The king was confined at Windsor, unable to comprehend that his son was to be married and certainly unable to attend the wedding.

With Edward, Duke of Kent, having recently married his wife, Victoria, Dowager Princess of Leiningen, at Amorbach in Bavaria, it was determined that the wedding at Kew would be a double one. The happy event on 11 July 1818 was one of the last occasions on which William and Victoria weren't at daggers drawn.

'Thursday was the day originally appointed for the marriage of the Duke of Clarence with the Princess Adelaide of Saxe Meiningen, and the re-marriage of the Duke and Duchess of Kent; but owing to the Queen's illness it was postponed, in order to enable her Majesty, if possible, to be present. Fortunately the Queen was so far better, as to be able to be present at the double ceremonial, for which purpose a temporary altar was fixed up in the Queen's drawing room which looks into Kew Gardens, and the ancient plate belonging to the Chapel Royal, &c. was used on the occasion. [...] The brides had the honour of being given away by the Prince Regent.'[49]

Both William and Adelaide had no illusions about the fact that their marriage must produce heirs and spares galore. You might expect given William's temper and Adelaide's unworldly ways that the marriage was a disaster, but you'd be mistaken. Adelaide's calm demeanour rubbed off on her new husband and as the Prince Regent continued to spend, spend, spend, she and William decided to leave England and live for a time in Hanover. Here they could enjoy a comparable but decidedly cheaper lifestyle, with the added benefit that William would be far away from any bad influences. Under Adelaide's steady guidance, he settled happily into the role of husband.

Though their union was a calm and loving one, it was beset with tragedy. Adelaide fell pregnant almost immediately and gave birth to a daughter, Charlotte, in March 1819. Sadly, Charlotte died within hours in what was to be the first of many such heartaches for the couple. Adelaide miscarried her second child in 1819 but in 1820, by now at home in London once more, she and William welcomed another daughter to the world, who they named Elizabeth. This, William was sure, signified a change in their fortune.

'I am this instant favoured with your kind note and congratulations on the safe delivery of the amiable and excellent Dutchess [sic]: the mother and infant thank God are going on as well as possible. I accept with sincere pleasure your wishes for the next being a boy: I have none little doubt [sic] but that the Dutchess will become a regular and fortunate mother.'[50]

Sadly, it was not to be. Elizabeth was born premature and suffered from a bowel disorder. For three months she was under the constant care of the finest royal physicians but despite their round the clock vigil, Elizabeth had a fit in the early hours of 4 March 1821. Adelaide was at her daughter's side when she passed away. She was distraught and together she and William sat beside the cradle of their little girl as they said their last goodbye. Adelaide fell pregnant just once more. She delivered stillborn twin boys in 1822 and though rumours continued to follow her, there were no more confirmed pregnancies.

The planned heirs were not to be.

King-in-Waiting

Though the duke and duchess continued to make regular trips back to Germany for the sake of their bank balance, ultimately, they made their home in England. William flirted with unpopularity in 1820 when, not long after the death of George III, his successor became determined to finally escape his marriage to Caroline of Brunswick. As George battled his hated wife, an apparently groundless rumour went around that William had attempted to arrange the seduction and ruin of Caroline, but all in all, life was quiet for the duke. By following Adelaide's sensible financial advice, he was even able to slowly chip away at his debts until they were relatively trifling.

In 1827, Frederick died. With that, William became first in line to the throne behind the gargantuan, alcohol and laudanum-riddled George IV. Whilst they were waiting for the Duke of York's funeral to begin in St George's Chapel at Windsor, William supposedly turned to his brother, the Duke of Sussex, and told him, 'We shall be treated *now*, Brother Augustus, very differently from what we have been.' In fact, William was almost the next into the grave and only narrowly avoided being flattened by a plummeting anchor-shaped chandelier at the Lord Mayor's Banquet that November.

Later that year, the prime minister, George Canning, appointed William Lord High Admiral. He was the first person to hold the post since 1709 and Canning hoped that the promotion would increase his standing in the favours of the heir to the throne. William had not lost his love of the ocean and he made tours of inspection on board his yacht, *The Royal Sovereign*. Adelaide was rather less fond of the seafaring life, so she followed the voyage by travelling along the coastline, making regular stops to see friends along the way. In the event, it was a position which William held for less than eighteen months, but one in which he quickly made several important changes. Just as Frederick had attempted to reform the army, so too did William try to do the same for sailors. He put a new focus on monitoring the condition and readiness of every ship in the British fleet and attempted to improve morale by outlawing use of the cat o'nine tails for anything other than mutiny. He clashed repeatedly with Admiralty officials due to his unauthorised spending and in July 1828, commandeered a fleet at Plymouth and simply disappeared. Upon his return from his impromptu voyage over a week later, William was asked to resign by the king and prime minister, the Duke of Wellington. He complied.

By now sure that he would one day wear the crown, William was happy to mark time. Despite the opposition of his fearsome brother, Ernest Augustus, Duke of Cumberland, he supported the Catholic Emancipation Bill, and remained a close companion of his eldest brother as his health failed. For most of his life William had never expected to be king but now, faced with George's ill health and the dwindling line of succession that had placed him right at its head, the most unlikely scenario was coming true.

At his home in Bushy House, William received regular reports on the condition of George IV from the king's secretary, Sir William Knighton. He kept up an almost daily correspondence with both Knighton and the Duke of Wellington, no doubt feeling anxious for George's health but also nervous excitement for the inevitable march towards his own coronation. Though we shouldn't doubt that William wished no ill on his brother, he was passing each day in expectation of 'that event which would involve me in particular, and the empire at large, in grief for the loss of the best and most amiable of monarchs.'[51]

In fact, William's nervous energy hadn't gone unnoticed by either Wellington or Tory Sir Henry Cooke. Cooke told a friend that '[Wellington] had abstained from all intercourse of a political character with the Duke of Clarence; treating with manifest coldness all such approaches on the part of the Duke of Clarence's friends or agents, as might bear the influence of intrigue. [I] will inform you now that the general bet is, that it is even chance that Clarence is in a straight-waistcoat before the King dies.'[52]

The general bet was to prove mistaken.

The Sailor King

At 6.00 am on 26 June 1830, William was awakened at Bushy House and told that his brother was dead. He was now King William IV of the United Kingdom.

'At twelve o'clock on Saturday the King was sworn in as William the Fourth, at his palace in St. James's. At half past eleven o'clock his Majesty, accompanied by her Excellent Majesty Queen Adelaide, arrived from Bushy-park [sic] at St James's Palace, in their private travelling carriage. Soon after their arrival the Archbishop of Canterbury and the Bishop of London proceeded to the palace and had an audience of his Majesty, to whom they administered the oaths taken by the Sovereign on his accession to the throne.

[…]

The King's Palace has, since his Majesty's arrival, been actually besieged with the carriages of the nobility and gentry hastening to pay their homage to the new King.'[53]

Having spent so long waiting to become king, William IV hit the ground running. Beside him was his son, George, who was to serve as his aide-de-camp. Well aware that one of the things that had caused the public to turn against his predecessor was the late king's dedication to largesse, William was seen as a welcome relief from that decadence by his new subjects. What he wanted, rather endearingly, was to make people happy. He did this by holding a relatively humble coronation, in contrast to the vast pageantry of George IV, and by doing all he could to prove that he was a man of the people.

William could often be seen strolling unattended in public and held events such as public feasts and entertainments that were for the benefit of the poorer members of society. Unlike George, who revelled in grandeur and adoration, William was a far less egotistical sort of fellow. He dismissed George's expensive continental chefs and replaced them with more affordable and less fancy homegrown cooks. When his friends came to visit, he brushed away any ceremony or formal dress and personally waved them off from the door. Adelaide likewise had no wish to be a glittering queen and together they tried to live a relatively normal life. William was capable of sensitivity too and personally invited Maria Fitzherbert to place her household in mourning following the death of George IV. Of course, she complied.

Diarist Charles Greville commented that 'he seems a kind-hearted, well-meaning, not stupid, burlesque, bustling old fellow, and if he doesn't go mad may make a very decent King, but he exhibits oddities.'[54] By the standards of George III, of course, those oddities were scarcely worth worrying about. One thing that *didn't* endear William to the public were his efforts to secure honours and titles for his children by Dora Jordan. As Greville wryly noted, 'the bastards are dissatisfied that more is not done for them, but he cannot do much for them at once, and he must have time.'[55] Ultimately the oldest of those so-called bastards, George, was to become estranged from his father thanks to worsening mental health problems that eventually caused him to take his life[56].

Yet for a man who was at pains to please, there was another challenging shadow lurking on the horizon. The Reform Crisis would test the new king to the limit.

The Reform Crisis

During the long eighteenth century, the death of a monarch and the succession of a new ruler was always followed by an election. At the ballot held in 1830, Wellington's Tories retained their majority, though they suffered substantial losses to Earl Grey's Whigs. The Tories were riven by infighting and when Wellington was cast out of power by a vote of no confidence in November 1830, Grey took his place as prime minister.

Returning to power for the first time in nearly 30 years, the new administration inherited a country that was heaving with distrust and anger. The Reform Act was intended to completely redraw the electoral system of the country in an attempt to quash malpractice and dishonesty and to ensure that the House of Commons was filled with members who had the real interests of their constituents at heart. The act would abolish rotten boroughs and increase suffrage by half a million voters but when the vote on its adoption took place, it was carried by a majority of just one. In order to carry the bill through, the Whigs recognised that they needed a greater majority in Parliament. In short, they needed another General Election.

Hungry for reform, the electorate returned the Whigs with a massive majority and reduced their opponents to a handful of mostly rotten boroughs. This time when the Reform Bill came before the house, they voted convincingly in favour of it. From there, the Bill was sent to the House of Lords. So great was the public's appetite for reform that there was a belief that the Bill's opponents in the Lords would abstain from voting rather than incur the wrath of the people. Instead they turned out in force and voted the Bill down.

Across the country, violent riots erupted. Because the same bill couldn't be debated twice in one session, the Lords had effectively smothered the Reform Bill, but Lord Grey wasn't done yet. When he asked William to prorogue Parliament, the king initially resisted but he changed his mind when he learned that Lord Wharncliffe intended to give an address opposing dissolution in the Lords. William took this as a personal attack on his authority and on 22 April 1831, declared his intention to go straight to the House of Lords and prorogue Parliament. It was a decision taken in such haste that it initially appeared as though he might have to travel in a hackney cab.

William arrived at the House of Lords as Wharncliffe's motion was being discussed. The scenes in the house were shocking to behold, with tempers and voices raised and even threats of violence. Lord Londonderry had to be physically restrained from literally whipping the supporters of the Whig cause. William's arrival stunned an already inflamed chamber, and he was in full regal flight when he strode into the chamber with his crown on his head.

'My Lords and Gentlemen,' William told the Lords as he began his prorogation speech, 'I have come to meet you for the purpose of proroguing this Parliament, with a view to its immediate dissolution [...]

I have been influenced only by a desire, and personal anxiety, for the contentment and happiness of my subjects.'

The country was still in turmoil when William attended his low-key coronation later that year. New to the job, he was already learning just how difficult life could really be for the king. Faced with a Commons that wanted reform and a Lords that bitterly opposed it, the new king was forced to realise that keeping people happy wasn't as easy as it looked.

'His Majesty opened the Parliament, on Tuesday, in person, and the leading topic of his Speech was Reform, of which his Majesty thus spoke:- "I feel it to be my duty , in the first place, to recommend to your most careful consideration the measures which will be proposed to you for a Reform in the Commons House of Parliament. A speedy and satisfactory settlement of this question becomes daily of more pressing importance to the security of the State, and to the contentment and welfare of the people.'[57]

After the Lords rejected the Reform Bill again, Grey suggested that they might be able to force it through if they stuffed the Upper House with new Whig lords who were sympathetic to reform. William, once an ardent Whig, put politics aside and rejected such a step in a bid to assert his royal power. Throughout the spring of 1832 the so-called Days of May crisis gripped the nation as protests broke out again, leading some to fear that the country stood on the brink of revolution. With William recoiling from Grey's requests to create new peerages, the prime minister resigned. William immediately offered the position to Wellington, but the Whig majority made his administration untenable, leaving William with no choice but to reappoint Grey and bow to his wishes. The king was backed into a corner. He warned that if the Lords continued to stifle reform, he would create new peers and leave the Upper House to deal with the possible consequences. This time the opponents of reform stood down. After a hard-fought battle, the Reform Act received the Royal Assent on 7 June 1832.

When William prorogued Parliament, it gave his popularity a massive boost and enhanced his image as a down-to-earth king who was willing to take on the Lords for the sake of the people. That didn't last. By not agreeing to Grey's demands it appeared that William had deliberately acted to halt the progress of reform. That wasn't the case. What William had intended was to assert his own power and show Lord Grey that he couldn't be pressured into taking decisions that he didn't agree with. Instead, the inexperienced sovereign received a bitter lesson in the workings of the British Parliament.

The Reform Act has been heralded as the birth of modern democracy. It was, as one newspaper put it, 'a bloodless revolution'[58], and the temporary cost to William's popularity was high. Queen Adelaide was a Tory traditionalist who opposed reform and eventually the blame for the king's reluctance to obey Grey's demands began to shift to her. When the press reminded readers that 'the Germans [have] sunk into thraldom,'[59] the implication was clear: Adelaide had leaned on her husband to frustrate the Reform Act. That wasn't the case[60]. Parliament had shown the sovereign just how unforgiving and downright difficult it could be. It was a lesson the king did well to learn, but it wasn't his last tangle with Westminster.

Though one might think William IV had had his fill of politics, he took an interest in the flashpoint that was religion. He wholeheartedly believed that it was the sovereign's duty to protect the established church and he balked at Earl Grey's enthusiasm for the Irish Church Temporalities Bill, which slashed the number of bishoprics controlled by the wealthy but relatively small Church of Ireland and abolished the system of tithes which had made the church far richer than its meagre size might suggest. Things took a radical turn when Lord John Russell voiced a plan to divert some of the Irish church's finances for lay matters, a proposal that horrified William.

When Lord Althorp inherited a peerage in late 1834 and moved to the Lords, prime minister Lord Melbourne decided to replace him as Leader of the House with Lord John Russell. Russell had been one of the loudest advocates for reform and this proposed promotion was a step too far for William. He dismissed the entire ministry – the last monarch to do so – and handed power to Sir Robert Peel, a Tory. His first term was short-lived and after four months of struggling against the Whig majority, Peel resigned. Melbourne returned to office and brought Russell with him to serve as Leader of the House. The days of the monarch commanding Parliament were well and truly done with.

The Pensioner's Stones

Just a couple of weeks after the Reform Bill received the royal assent, William visited Ascot. As he watched the racing from the grandstand, a man threw two large stones, one of which hit him square in the forehead. William reeled back and exclaimed, 'Oh God! I am hit!', but luckily old Coconut Head had taken to padding his hats to make them fit more snugly on his unusually shaped cranium. That padding protected him from serious injury, but he was still badly shaken. As the king and queen took cover, their attacker was detained and taken for questioning at Bow Street.

The man revealed himself to be a native of Cork named Dennis Collins, who was in his fifties. He was a pitiful figure who wore the tattered remains of a naval uniform and hobbled on a wooden leg. Collins explained that he had served in the navy for many years and had lost his leg after suffering an accident on board the *Atalanta*. He had a fresh but minor head wound too, sustained when some members of the public were rather too keen in their attempts to detain him. He smelled of beer but was sober and lucid.

Collins explained that, having lost his leg in the service of his country, he was admitted as a pensioner to Greenwich Hospital, where he remained until December 1831, when he was unceremoniously kicked out. The cause of his removal was unfair, he claimed, as he had merely asked the ward-keeper to sweep the ward no more than once each day. When another pensioner remonstrated with Collins, it turned into an argument. As a result, Collins was turned out and his pension was stopped. Since then, Collins had lived as a vagrant, with no money and no prospects. He had petitioned the Lords of the Admiralty and the king himself for assistance but had received none. When he visited an admiral to ask for help, he was physically assaulted. This had been the final straw.

Although his petition to the monarch had been left at Whitehall, Collins was convinced that William had personally ignored his plea for help. So furious was the veteran that he determined to find the king at Ascot and stone him. Starving, homeless and hopeless, he decided that he 'might as well be shot or hanged as remain in such a state.' Collins had been detained at Bow Street for minor misdemeanours before and this time he was taken to Reading Jail to await trial.

On 22 August, Collins pleaded not guilty to a charge of high treason. He remorsefully told the court that 'His Majesty never did me an injury. [...] I can only say I am very sorry for what I have done and must suffer the law. They had no right to take my pension from me, to which I was entitled by Act of Parliament.'[61]

The verdict was guilty. The pensioner was sentenced to be drawn and quartered, but mercifully his sentence was commuted to transportation. Dennis Collins was sent to Van Deiman's Land, where he died the following year. His pension, of course, was never restored.

Family Affairs

William's brushes with politics had left him battered, but he was bruised further by the mere presence of his sister-in-law, Victoria, Duchess of Kent, with whom he had shared a double wedding. In her, William saw an ambitious social climber who was readying herself for the death of the elderly king. In short, everything that his own beloved Adelaide was not. The duchess believed that the day she longed for would come sooner rather than later, and when it did, her own daughter, Victoria, would be queen. If that was the case, Victoria would inherit the crown before she reached her majority and who better to serve as all-powerful Regent than her own career-minded mother?

William was equally determined to outlive the duchess. He disapproved of her strict and isolating parenting methods and the influence of John Conroy, the comptroller who ran her household and was very likely her lover too. The duchess, meanwhile, believed that William was an immoral idiot. She tried to keep Victoria from meeting her uncle too often and even moved herself and the little princess into the nicest rooms that Kensington Palace had to offer, rooms that had been renovated and reserved for the king and queen themselves. If that weren't enough, the duchess simply refused to acknowledge the king's children with Dora Jordan and for William, that was beyond the pale.

William's relationship with his illegitimate offspring wasn't always perfect, but he loved them. When his eldest son, George, began to suffer increasingly violent mood swings and demanded ever more money and prestige, William initially tried to ignore the advice of his courtiers that he must see less of his son. Yet as the confrontations became ever more vicious and upsetting for the elderly king, he reluctantly agreed not to see his son. It was an agonising decision.

Yet still William was determined to live on, if only to frustrate the Duchess of Kent. As young Princess Victoria approached her eighteenth birthday, he made a shockingly honest public address to a feast at which the duchess was present.

> 'I trust to God that my life may be spared for nine months longer [...] I should then have the satisfaction of leaving the exercise of the Royal authority to the personal authority of that young lady, heiress presumptive to the Crown, and not in the hands of a person now near me, who is surrounded by evil advisers and is herself incompetent to act with propriety in the situation in which she would be placed.'

Only when the duchess fled the banquet in tears did William realise that this time, he had gone too far. Though they did manage to reach a mutual truce in the last months of his life, it was far from easy.

The king's spirits and health plummeted when his favourite daughter, Sophia, passed away in childbirth in April 1837. As Baroness De L'Isle and Dudley, she was the State Housekeeper of Kensington Palace and her death accelerated William's own decline. Just as George III had been overwhelmed when his own favourite, Amelia, had died, now William followed the same spiral. His asthma became worse than ever before, with severe and debilitating attacks occurring with alarming regularity. Soon he was under the watchful eye of the ever-present royal physicians.

By May 1837 William was still soldiering on, receiving his ministers and his doctors alike, alternating between bursts of energy and complete exhaustion. He was mostly confined to a wheelchair but if his health was faltering, his spirits and wits were sharp. Throughout early June he became progressively weaker and Queen Adelaide remained devotedly at his side day and night, praying with him or simply sitting with her husband as he slept. Though she tried to contain her composure, on one occasion the thought of her husband's illness left her in tears. William told her lightly, 'Bear up,' as though he was suffering from nothing worse than a cold. When he welcomed each of his surviving children in turn to say farewell, both William and Adelaide knew that he was preparing for the end.

'It has pleased Almighty God to release from his suffering our Most Excellent and Gracious Sovereign King William the Fourth.

His Majesty expired at twelve minutes past two o'clock a.m. this day.'[62]

For ten days Adelaide remained with William. She was holding his hand when he died in the early hours of 20 June 1837, at the age of 71.[63] His last words were, 'the church, the church.'

The Sailor King got his last wish. Princess Victoria had celebrated her eighteenth birthday on 24 May and though he had been too unwell to attend her party, William had lived long enough to ensure that her mother would never be Regent. With its naval adventures and romantic entanglements, gambling debts and days at the races, William IV's life was quintessentially Georgian. Yet he was also present at the birth of a new kind of democracy, one that we still recognise today. Though reformers felt that he wasn't radical enough and anti-reformers believed that he had too much zeal for his own good, both failed to recognise that ultimately, he aimed to find a middle ground. It was an honourable if naïve goal, but this down-to-earth monarch was no match for the wiles of men who had lived their whole lives at the forefront of British politics.

Still, as William himself commented, 'I have my view of things, and I tell them to my ministers. If they do not adopt them, I cannot help it. I have done my duty.'

And what more could he do than that?

Edward, Duke of Kent and Strathearn
(2 November 1767–23 January 1820)

The Fourth Son

'Yesterday there was a very numerous Levee at St. James's, when his
Majesty received the compliments of the Nobility, &c. on the happy
delivery of the Queen, and the birth of a Prince.

We are assured that her Majesty and the young Prince continues
as well as can be expected, but her Majesty as yet sees no company,
except the Ladies of the Bed Chamber, and the Maids of Honour.'[1]

Prince Edward was the fourth son and fifth child of George III and
Charlotte of Mecklenburg-Strelitz. Though his fame has been eclipsed
by that of his only legitimate child, Queen Victoria, Edward enjoyed
plenty of notoriety of his own in his day. He was named in honour of his
paternal uncle, the Duke of York and Albany, whose funeral had taken
place just the day before the new prince was born.

On the whole, fourth sons have very little chance of inheriting the
crown. The search for an identity of their own had led George III's
brothers into indolence and scandal and the king was determined that
his son wouldn't suffer the same fate. As Edward sat for his portrait at St
James's in November 1769, his father was already considering the little
prince's future.

In the short term, that meant business as usual. There was to be no
change in the routine of the royal schoolroom that had already churned
out George, Frederick, and William, and Edward was the next boy to
enter the well-rehearsed system. Just like his brothers he was supervised
by Lord Holderness and just as George and Frederick had been tutored
as a pair, so would Edward join William at his lessons.

Edward, however, was not the hardiest child, even if he bounced back
from his smallpox inoculation in 1770 with scarcely any complaint.

Everything seemed to be going like clockwork, but as we have learned, that was usually the point at which things started to go wrong. Edward might have been safe from smallpox, but his childhood health was always considerably weaker than that of his elder brothers and in October 1771, he was laid low by whooping cough. In fact, the health of the royal children deteriorated with each new birth and in some ways, Edward was the start of the slow but steady decline. To improve his strength, Edward learned to swim, assured that 'seabathing makes us much stronger. I am now able to jump in by myself, tho' at first I did not relish it much.'[2] Within five years, after battling one episode of ill health after another, the sickly little boy was dancing at royal balls.

The little prince made his first public appearance alongside William just a week before his eighth birthday. Though his elder brothers and sisters had made their debuts at that ill-conceived drawing room, resplendent in ceremonial garb and roman togas, Charlotte wisely decided to forego any set dressing on this occasion. Instead the children were merely presented at the drawing room, they didn't go so far as to actually host it.

Prince Edward was growing up and his Victorian-era biographer catalogued an incident which more than any other seems to show his character. It involved a clock that was one of George III's most treasured possessions, having once belonged to the short-lived son of Queen Anne. One morning the palace servants at Kew found the clock smashed to pieces on the floor, completely irreparable. The furious king demanded to know who had committed the outrage, but nobody held their hand up. Eventually, hours later, Prince Edward was asked if he could throw any light on the subject. Though nobody would have been any the wiser had he pretended to know nothing, he instead said straightaway, 'I did it.'

When asked if it was an accident, Edward said that it wasn't, he had smashed the clock intentionally. His tutor, John Fisher, asked if he was sorry and the prince replied, 'No; I may be sorry for it to-morrow, but I certainly am not sorry for it now.' Though his motive went unspoken, the king punished him severely for the act of vandalism. Fisher believed that the incident perfectly demonstrated the defining characteristic of his youthful charge. Honesty, above everything.

'The boy was father to the man. In this trait of character lies the secret of many of the after sorrows of his life. With him truth was omnipotent. *He could not dissemble* Were those, who in a measure controlled his destiny, able justly to estimate his character? *Could* they appreciate it? *Did* they? I fear not.'[3]

A Young Soldier

In 1780, King George appointed John Fisher to serve as his son's preceptor or teacher, overseeing his education and becoming a lifelong friend. Fisher, a future Bishop of Salisbury, was a keen amateur artist[4] and his passion rubbed off on his young charge. Though Edward's talent for art was further nurtured by lessons from painter Alexander Cozens, there was no way that his father would allow him to languish as an artist or a musician, which was his other passion. Instead, the forces beckoned.

As we've seen in the cases of Frederick and William, George was determined that his sons should spend their adolescence in Germany. Here they would complete their education and be prepared to serve their countries. At first, he toyed with the idea of sending Edward to the University of Göttingen and asked Frederick for his opinion on the matter. After all, who better to quiz on the lie of the land?

Frederick, the acknowledged favourite and wisest son, had his reservations. If their father wanted Edward to be properly watched and kept in line during his education, then Göttingen was *not* the place to be.

'[Frederick's tutors] agree with me in the idea that though certainly Edward might find better and more famous masters there than at Lunebourg, yet there is one circumstance that does not appear to have struck those who have recommended Gottingen [sic] to your Majesty, which is, that one cannot judge of Gottingen or indeed of any other German University by an English one, where the young men are confined in Colleges and the tutors have a great authority over them. At Gottingen, on the contrary, the young men all live separately, and the Professors have very little more than a nominal authority over them, so that there does not pass a day without some very great excess or other being committed. We therefore humbly submit it to your Majesty if it would not be very risking to send a young man who has never been in the world before to such a place, where he shall hear every day of these excesses and where he will in a manner be obliged to keep company with the very people who commit them. And if unluckily he was to take this turn, being at an age not to be treated like a child, it would be very difficult to keep him back.'5

While it might have suited Edward to be able to run wild, it wasn't exactly what the king was planning for his son. For a time, both Frederick and George continued to research the university but essentially Frederick's words of warning had already torpedoed the idea. The king had had enough of troublesome sons with George, Prince of Wales, and the last thing he needed was Edward going off the rails in Hanover. His mind was made up.

In 1785 Edward travelled to Lüneburg and joined the Hanoverian Guards, where he rose to the rank of Colonel within a year. Once a wealthy town, Lüneburg had slumped into poverty and when Edward saw it, he felt thoroughly miserable. To make matters worse, he was to trade the relatively gentle companionship of the godly Fisher for the stern company of Lieutenant Colonel Baron George von Wangenheim, whom he described as 'a mercenary tyrant.' Wangenheim was put in charge of Edward's annual allowance of £1,000 and he was permitted to charge certain expenses to it too, on condition that they were incurred in his role as Edward's guardian. Even though he had his own salary of £6,000, Wangenheim was soon practising some very creative accounting, dipping into the allowance in a way that Edward furiously described as 'open robbery.'

Of course, there was nothing the young man could do about it. Instead he swallowed his rage and submitted to his new life, repeating the same endless routine of parades and drills for twelve stultifying months. Within no time, he had requested a relocation to Hanover, but George believed that what his son needed could be ably provided in the less glamorous surroundings of Lüneburg. Instead, all he succeeded in doing was making freedom more tempting than ever. Spirited from Kew to his military career, Edward knew that there was a life out there to be lived. When he attempted to complain about the situation to the king, his letters were censored by Wangenheim or disappeared altogether. Desperate, he enlisted the help of his brother. Frederick wrote to inform George that:

'[Edward] was at first rather a little wild, but now he seems to have settled very well to his studies and to apply himself very much. He desired me to intercede with your Majesty on his behalf, in order that he might soon be placed in the Army. If I may be allowed to give my opinion this favour would be of very great use in spiriting him on to apply himself and make him feel more and more that his advancement depends totally upon his forming himself to be useful to his country.'[6]

The king could ignore Edward's pleas, but he was far more likely to listen to Frederick. Edward might have stood for a lot, but in common with his brothers, he wouldn't stand for living in anything other than the best royal style. If Wangenheim wouldn't give him the cash, then he decided that he would borrow it instead. Without the knowledge of his brothers or Wangenheim, the prince approached people who 'were so very absurd as to give Edward credit to any amount that he pleased, and even to offer to lend him as much money as he wanted.'[7] Edward took the cash with no hope of paying it back and spent it on his quarters and even the musicians of his garrison.

It was a bad start in life and one that Edward himself later rued, for he never learned how to live within his means. When the king discovered what Edward had done, he feared that it was the start of a slippery and debt-ridden slope. Although he granted Edward's wish to be transferred to Hanover and even settled his accounts, George was not a happy man. Perhaps in an effort to prick his father's conscience just a little, Edward wrote from his new billet to tell him that he had narrowly escaped a horrible fate when the axle of his phaeton snapped and he was dragged along the ground by the horses. He sustained only minor injuries. Certainly nothing that would curb his spending.

In Hanover and by now a Knight of the Garter, at least Edward could be watched far more closely by Frederick, who approved of Wangenheim's influence despite his brother's objections. George now received quarterly reports on Edward's finances from his miserly guardian, but the young man was very keen to prove that he had changed his ways. More than that, he was desperate to take charge of his own finances and to wrest his money from the grip of Wangenheim, but George was having none of it.

So, Edward started borrowing again. When the king discovered what his son had done, he was furious. If he was angry at the first lot of debts, he was apoplectic at the second.

'After the strong & repeated assurances you gave me in writing on my relieving your debts, […] it is easy to conceive how much I am offended at your having not only continued the same shameful conduct, but by those assurances shewn you have wilfully and knowingly added untruths to the former errors. Nay, the pay of Colonel has been employed in futile addition to the Band of Musick and Drummers of the Regiment, contrary to the regulations laid down by me in that service, and the other expences [sic] have been incurred by building, altering and changing carriages, besides buying and keeping horses unknown to me and contrary to my express orders. I have allowed you the use of my carriages, and of sufficient horses for your use, to which you have added all those which you must've known when once come to my knowledge would incurr [sic] my highest approbation. [I have therefore ordered] that every addition of musicians, drummers, or any other article in the Guards that you have added […] be instantly discharged and no innovation of the most trifling kind permitted. I cannot keep up a due subordination unless I make the world see my sons must not presume to alter any regulations I have made. [In addition,] all the carriages you have bought, & the horses must instantly be sold, and any servants you have engaged […] must be discharged. I should have flattered myself that the having placed you in the Army would have opened your ideas & have drawn you from spending your time in a manner so much below you. […] But to try if it be not possible to put some ideas into you more becoming of your birth & station, I will instantly send you on your travels.'[8]

Of course, all of this rather flies in the face of Fisher's belief that nothing was more important to Edward than the truth, but perhaps the story of the clock offers us another glimpse into his character. He didn't confess to smashing the clock until he was asked if it was him. In this case, nobody asked Edward if he was borrowing money and spending it on living the high life, so he simply didn't tell them. When Edward responded to his father's furious letter, he told George that, though he was ashamed of his behaviour, he wouldn't make any further promises because his father quite rightly wouldn't believe them. Instead he simply confirmed that he had sold his carriages and horses and dismissed everyone that he had appointed. That done, he appealed to the king, 'on my knees, addressing you as my Sovereign & as my father, to implore your pardon for my past improper conduct, & to express how anxiously I wish to regain your gracious favour, which I have now had the misfortune to lose.'[9] There was one thing more precious to Edward than honesty: the approval of his father.

Escape to Scandal

Forced to sell his finery and dismiss his servants, the now 20-year-old Edward was humiliated. With such an obvious and embarrassing rift between king and prince and the humiliation of having to sell off his possessions, Edward's position in the Hanoverian army had become untenable and George decided instead to send him to Geneva to enter into a strict academic programme. Here, the king hoped that his son would learn to behave in a manner better befitting a prince, but he and his offspring always had wildly different interpretations of what that behaviour should be.

Edward harboured no resentment towards his father for any of this but directed his anger at Wangenheim instead. He believed that if his guardian had shown more generosity with his allowance, then he wouldn't be in this embarrassing situation, let alone at loggerheads with the king. Edward was desperate to win back George's approval, believing that 'there is none of all your sons who is more devotedly attached to you than I am,' and he truly believed it. These weren't empty words, but a beseeching desire for approval from a son who longed for 'the good opinion and the favor [sic] of his father and his Sovereign' above all. When George granted him a new phaeton, an allowance of £6,000 and the rank of colonel in the 7th Regiment of Foot (Royal Fusiliers), it was the sign of trust slowly being restored.

Recognising that if he was to be part of the English army, then he really ought to be in England, Edward asked his father for permission to surrender his rank of Corporal in the Hanoverian Guards and come home to Great Britain. Though he framed it as a matter of duty, such a move would allow the prince to escape Wangenheim, who he had come to regard as a 'bearkeeper'.

Wangenheim didn't keep quite as close an eye on Edward as he might have thought though, because Edward followed the lesson set by his brothers and added women to his list of interests. Chief among them was a musician named Adelaide Dubus. She was six years his senior and was soon pregnant with Edward's first child. Adelaide died delivering a daughter named Adelaide Victoria August, who was born when Edward was about 22, and was entrusted to the care of her late mother's sister.

With the death of his lover, Edward's Swiss adventure soured. He took stock of his broken heart, his bad credit and his bearkeepers and asked again if he could come back to England. When the king's permission wasn't forthcoming, Edward decided to leave under his own steam. Wangenheim learned of the plan and wrote to George to ask him to intervene, but it was far too late.

'[It] appears more and more from the arrangements secretly made by His Royal Highness Prince Edward that it is his intention to set out for England,'[10] Wangenheim warned, urging the king to take immediate action to prevent the prince from fleeing. Yet by the time the baron's letter reached England, Edward was already on his way.

How Edward hadn't guessed that such a dramatic stand was a fatal error beggars belief, but in January 1790, he stole away from Geneva and hastened towards the coast. Through the harsh winter he fled, accompanied only by a *Mr Sturt*, son of the Member of Parliament for Dorset, and when he landed in England and made for Nerot's Hotel in St James's, the gossip mill went into overdrive. Almost immediately, the press published a breathless account of the return of the prince, who now stood at well over six feet in height, and it speculated at the cause of his unexpected change of circumstances. There could be no other explanation for his flight from Geneva than heartbreak, the press decided, and the desperation of a grieving man.

'An incident of a pathetic nature operated in a degree to induce him to leave Geneva; a young lady, of French birth, is said to have engaged a share of his attachment, and after an intimacy of some duration, she appeared in a state of pregnancy.

Her death happened a short time since; she died in child-bed and left a charming little girl behind her. During her indisposition, the unremitted care and solicitation, shewn by her admirer, demonstrated a heart rich in the finest feeling of nature.'[11]

The return of the prince was far from that imagined by the idealistic journalists of the *Argus*. They dismissed any idea that Edward would face punishment and instead tried to imagine what joy his unexpected return must have brought to the royal household. They couldn't have been more wrong.

'[It] is easier to conceive than describe the emotions of parental joy, which so unexpected a visit excited in the Royal bosoms.

The presence of this new visitor at Court, on her MAJESTY's Birth-day, may help to disperse the gloom which may be occasioned by the absence and indisposition of two of his Royal brothers.'[12]

When Edward sought an audience with his father, it wasn't forthcoming. George was still fragile after a bout of ill health and he was fuming at Edward's audacious return to the fold. Instead the Prince of Wales collected Edward from the hotel and brought him to his old rooms at St James's Palace. There he was to remain whilst his father ruminated on what could be done with him. Though Edward was permitted to visit his elder brothers, he was forbidden from seeing his parents, sisters or younger siblings. Make no mistake, the king was furious. He met with his ministers and discussed what the appropriate course of action would be for a son who had proven time and again that he simply wouldn't learn.

But Edward hadn't fled Geneva lightly. Though all we can judge him by is his letters, one can't help but feel that he meant every promise he made to do better. Yet he had been hurried from a strict childhood to Europe and there placed in the charge of a disciplinarian who, fatally, he simply didn't respect. Wangenheim frustrated and antagonised Edward, rightly or wrongly, and when his requests for a little more freedom or money were ignored or rebuffed, he did what innumerable young men and women have done since time immemorial: he kicked back twice as hard. We need only imagine Wales' and Frederick's roistering in London or William's snowy parties in New York to see that the royal princes were popular wherever they went, and Edward was no different. He enjoyed flattery and loved to be the centre of attention, so the more money he spent on his friends and comrades, the more they cheered him on. He had been away from England for years when he fled from Geneva and he did so only when his requests for leave to come home had been ignored. It's certainly not an excuse, but for a young man who was still being treated like a naughty boy, it's hardly surprising that he had reached his limit.

It's hardly surprising too that the king didn't take it lightly. He wasn't particularly close to Edward to begin with, as he had repeatedly fallen short of his father's idea of a perfect royal son. George's refusal to see Edward was a technique favoured by Queen Charlotte when she wanted to punish her daughters: the royal couple understood the devastating power of isolation. Though George might not grant his son an audience, behind the scenes, he was the topic of much debate between the king and Pitt. Within days, they had decided that the best thing to do was to return Edward to the army and give him the job of bringing the notorious Queen's Royal Regiment back under control. He would be dispatched to Gibraltar immediately. Perhaps the king hoped that on the distant Rock, Edward would escape the influence of his profligate and flattering friends. If nothing else, it would get him away from London.

George III finally agreed to an audience with Edward on the evening before his departure. It was over in minutes and was far from the heartfelt reconciliation envisioned by the *Argus*. Edward would spend the next few months writing letters to his father in which he promised, time and time again, to be a better son.

The Rock

Edward arrived on Gibraltar in the dying days of February 1790, determined to put right his many wrongs. With him were the Royal Fusiliers, the company he had been colonel of for a year and had been so keen to return to the United Kingdom to join. He was free of Wangenheim and in the care instead of Captain Charles Gregan Crauford, who had previously been an equerry to the Duke of York and who would become a good friend. This time, Edward was determined that he would make his father proud. So began one of the most controversial periods of the prince's life.

It was during his short tenure in Gibraltar that Edward gained a reputation for tyranny. In the years that followed this reputation never left him and he remains notorious as the prince who delighted in flogging his soldiers whenever they stepped out of line. Contrast this with William, who outlawed the use of the cat o'nine tails in all but the most extreme cases, then consider what a different personality he must have been. Yet in the rush to condemn Edward as a disciplinarian with a taste for sadism, we shouldn't lose sight of the fact that the methods he employed were not only common, but positively encouraged. Flogging wasn't something that only Edward used, barbaric though it may seem to us today.

George had hoped that sending his son to the military outpost of Gibraltar would focus his mind and so it did, though perhaps not as the king might have wished. True, Edward devoted himself to his duty and curbed his profligate ways, but he longed for companionship of a less soldierly sort. In a candid mood, he told Wales, 'I despise every sensual enjoyment, which one might procure when the object of it is a prostitute, in short, I look for a companion, not for a whore. I know, you will laugh at my strange out of the way ideas, but consult your own heard, and then reflect, with this sentiment, if it is possible for me to live solus very contented in a fortress like this, where, even those who love the bawdy house are obliged to practise much self-denial.'[13] George, who had married Mrs Fitzherbert in 1785, knew all about domestic longing.

Edward wouldn't settle for anything less than his own little home with all its attendant comforts, from a woman to keep him happy to a child with whom he could play as his own father had once done with him. Without any feminine company and with nothing but drunken soldiers and drill practice to occupy him, Edward's mind kept wandering back to Geneva and his late lover, not to mention Victoria, the caring sister who had taken in her niece. The more he thought about Victoria, the more attractive she seemed and eventually, he concluded that he simply must see her again. This time Edward didn't take off as he had from Switzerland, but instead sent for Victoria to join him in Gibraltar under the cover story that she was to provide some musical entertainment and give Edward the chance to meet his little girl. Sadly, the trip proved disastrous. Little Adelaide Victoria died during the voyage and Victoria proved to be far less enchanting than her late sister. Edward sent her back to France and, heavy of heart, languished on the Rock.

But Edward was lonely, so he dispatched his agent, Monsieur Fontiny, to the mainland to find a woman who would like to be the paramour of a prince. Fontiny lost no time in doing so and soon fate threw Alphonsine-Thérèse-Bernardine-Julie de Montgenêt de Saint-Laurent, better known to history simply as *Madame de Saint-Laurent*, into his path. Like all the best courtesans her history is patchy at best, and her life was a swirling fog of contradictions, half-truths and supposed husbands. Julie, as she was known, styled herself as Baroness Fortisson, but it's far more likely that Baron Fortisson was a patron to this career courtesan. Still, the title added a sheen of respectability to the adventuress who was described by one acquaintance as a woman of 'an [sic] hundred names and titles'. Fontiny saw in Julie the perfect candidate to make Edward's wishes come true, whilst for Julie, this lonely British prince was the next step on an illustrious career ladder.

Julie was seven years Edward's senior and just as many courtesans and gentlemen did in the era, they agreed what amounted to an employment contract. Julie would essentially be Edward's wife, though there would be no marriage, and he in return would provide her with a home, money and protection. Lest she had any illusions about the life she was about to enter into, he warned her that 'Having made your contract with a soldier, you must make up your mind to carry the knapsack and not dream of the broidered coverlets of kings and the great of this world.'[14] It was true, of course; well, certainly more true than his claims that '[my family] have no deeper wish than to win your friendship and offer you theirs.'[15] Fat chance.

Julie was to enter the garrison under the guise of a musician but once there, she became the chatelaine of the prince's heart. The relationship would last for years and, like that of George and Maria Fitzherbert or William and Dora Jordan, end only when duty came knocking.

The arrival of Julie threw Edward's guardians into a minor panic, but Edward and his lady would not be moved. They had a contract and they were determined to keep it. What the king made of all this is anyone's guess, but he had a peculiar talent for acceptance when it came to his sons' lovers. So long as there was no marriage, George had become adept at turning a blind eye and that was exactly what he did when it came to Julie. If Edward continued to avoid the gaming table and the moneylender, having a lady on his arm was the lesser of many possible evils.

Many reasons have been put forward for the king's unexpected decision to have his son moved from Gibraltar to Canada. Three have emerged as the chief theories and they are, briefly, to keep him away from Julie, to quash reports of his sadism, or simply on account of his poor health. The first we can discount, because Julie went to Canada too. Likewise, the second might have a whiff of the tabloids about it, but it's highly unlikely that George wouldn't have discussed such a matter in his correspondence. As for the third, whilst it might be the least scandalous, it's certainly the most likely. Edward wrote to his father and told him pitifully that:

'[My] health has so materially suffered during the immoderate heat of last summer that the Surgeon General of our Garrison, who has constantly attended me during the frequent bilious attacks from which I have felt the most violent and serious effects, has given it as his positive opinion that by my remaining here another summer season my health would be exposed not only to the most prejudicial but perhaps the most fatal attacks of a complaint, the severity of which is, I believe, not unknown to your Majesty.

[...]

[Nothing] would give me more pain than my being at present obliged to quit the Regiment I have now the honor [sic] of commanding. [I hope that] you will allow me to be sent in the Spring with [my Regiment] to any part of North America which you may chuse [sic] to appoint; allowing me, if it meets with your approbation, to prefer Canada. I trust my services in that part of your foreign dominions may perhaps be of more use than they could be my lingering with sickness in this.'[16]

Edward was wise to lean heavily on the argument of ill health, because it was a something that the king knew all about from his own bitter experience. Besides, this time, Edward wasn't simply asking to come home, but to be moved to somewhere where the summers might not prove so injurious to him, and he was willing to quit the army altogether if the answer was *no*. George wished his son no harm and, faced with his suffering, he gave the posting to Canada his seal of approval.

'I shall leave no means untried to dissuade his R. Highness from taking along with him the female who has lately joined him here – and which he seems at present resolved on,' wrote the garrison's Lieutenant Colonel, but Edward and Julie resisted every effort to part them. 'We must therefore look on it as an evil which at present possibly cannot be removed,' was the officer's conclusion, 'and act accordingly.'[17]

Edward and Julie left Gibraltar in May 1791 aboard HMS *Resistance*, after attending a grand ball thrown in the prince's honour. There was even a song to send him on his way, the voice of the young soloist echoing long into the Mediterranean night as the prince said goodbye to his garrison.

> 'For Royal Edward leaves us now!
> 'Twas he who taught us how to bear
> The soldier's toil, the leader's care;
> Yet cheer'd fatigue with festive hours,
> And strew'd War's rugged path with flow'rs.'

Canada

'His Royal Highness Prince EDWARD, has left Gibraltar, for America; his retinue when he sailed, was rather domestic than Princely; a French Lady, his own man, and a Swiss valet, composing his whole suite.'[18]

After an arduous seven-week voyage, Edward's ship anchored off Quebec. Might he have felt a pang of relief as he watched this new land emerge from the mist? Here was a new start, far away from his stultifying parents and the grim heat of Gibraltar. Canada was a British territory, though North America was now enjoying independence, and an uneasy mix of French majority and British minority, the two groups not so much cordial with one another as just about tolerant.

Edward's welcome to Quebec was a far cry from William's triumphant arrival in New York, let alone his high-spirited trip to Canada. Nobody was queuing up to take Edward skating or drinking and instead he was taken to meet the governor, Lord Dorchester, and representatives of the First Nations. This time, he was determined to make his father proud.

Julie and Edward set up home together on rue St Louis as though they were husband and wife. Yet Julie *wasn't* Edward's wife and for some, her inclusion in his household was a step too far. The political elite of Quebec was torn between politely but reluctantly including her in invitations, or simply pretending she didn't exist. For Lord Dorchester, the answer was simple. Though he wasn't exactly enamoured of the situation, Dorchester decided that discretion was the better part of valour and accepted Julie as a fact of life. It was probably the path of least resistance.

Edward soon embarked on a PR drive to win over the residents of Quebec, but he persevered with his belief that old-fashioned Hanoverian discipline was the way to build an army. This resulted in the desertion of at least one man, a respected French soldier named William La Rose, who had planned a rebellion with around a dozen of Edward's Royal Fusiliers. When his plan was discovered La Rose fled, only to be apprehended by Edward in a tavern. The rebel submitted to his arrest but told Edward that 'you are fortunate, my Lord, in my not being armed, for by Heaven, I if I had my pistol I would have blown out your brains.'

William La Rose was far from fortunate when it came to his court marital. Tried under the Mutiny Act, he revealed that he had planned to take his entire regiment south and hand it over to George Washington, with whom he had served during the American Revolution. He was sentenced to receive nine hundred and ninety-nine strokes of the lash, which did little to help Prince Edward's reputation for cruelty.

La Rose's fellow rebels were sentenced to punishments ranging from four hundred lashes to death. Joseph Draper, the only mutineer to receive the death sentence, was given a royal pardon thanks to a petition put to the king by his colonel, Prince Edward. Draper didn't receive his pardon until he had taken part in his own execution procession, when the despairing man followed behind his coffin to the accompaniment of a funereal dirge. Despite this last-minute show of mercy, the punishments meted out sent a clear message to any other soldiers who might be thinking about resisting the prince's methods. The episode also reignited those accusations of unnecessarily sadistic discipline that had previously dogged him.

Edward wasn't unpopular with everyone, perhaps because some of his initiatives were philanthropic. He became the patron of a Sunday Free School to which anyone was invited. Here children would learn reading, writing and arithmetic, taught in both English and French, though with an eye to ensuring that the French students learned to speak English, rather than the other way around. He even joined Lord Dorchester to fight a domestic fire, which further added to their *men of the people* image.

The prince enjoyed getting to know his new territory, but he still harboured hopes of returning to England before he had to face the Canadian winter. He roamed and explored during the day and came home to Julie at night, finding her the perfect companion. They were soon an integral part in the social fabric of the city and in London, the king breathed a sigh of relief. Well aware that his son had made every effort to pay off his outstanding European debts during his time in Gibraltar, he could see the very real attempts Edward was making to put right his wrongs. Regardless of their legal status as a couple, Julie was a calming influence. For once, all seemed suspiciously peaceful.

By this point, Edward had been away from home for eight years with only one impromptu stopover in London. He had paraded and practised and drilled and wanted nothing more than to finally see some action. What better opportunity than the war against France? Once again, he wrote to the king to beg for permission to come home and, mindful that Wales also longed for action, Edward wrote to him too. He begged his brother to support him and promised that he would happily join another regiment if that meant a swift call to arms. This wasn't a matter of bluster or ego either, but a desperate wish to serve his country. It was a desire to do his duty that he had inherited from his troubled father.

The Prince of Wales did what he could. He made representations to the king on behalf of Edward but for months, the younger prince was held in a state of nervous excitement and inactivity. He had spent years preparing, had toed the line in Quebec and swore that '[I] have not a desire to loiter one moment in London, [I] am ready faithfully to engage.' It wasn't only Wales and Edward who thought he was ready for action either. Henry Dundas, Minister for War, had 'no hesitation in giving my decided opinion [that] the Prince should be gratified in his wishes of serving either in the conquest of the West India Islands or in the south of France.' Accordingly, in October 1793, the king gave his consent. He agreed to have Edward promoted to the rank of Major General and sent to the West Indies, where a conflict had broken out as part of the French Revolutionary Wars. Edward was placed under the command of General Sir Charles Grey.

Finally able to put his training into practice, Edward flourished in the campaign to bring the French-controlled islands under British rule. As Julie left for London, the prince hopped aboard a sleigh and crossed the snowy Canadian wilderness, battling harsh conditions every step of the way. At one point two of the sleighs in the party plunged through the frozen surface of Lake Champlain, taking with them all the prince's clothes and a good deal of valuable property. It was a cruel blow to Edward, who had been managing his finances reasonably well in Canada, and the loss of his bags to that frozen lake would have cost him a fortune.

When Edward arrived in Boston, the ship he had been expecting to meet there had already sailed. Instead he waited for a rather less grand vessel to finally take him into the heart of the action in the West Indies. There he found himself in the midst of a brutal and short campaign from which the British swiftly emerged victorious, and Edward certainly did his bit. Though impressed with his youthful vigour, Lord Grey was mindful that losing a Prince of the Blood in the heat of battle wouldn't exactly cover him in glory. He praised Edward's dedication and courage, whilst counselling him to be more cautious when it came to the frontline. Edward enjoyed success after success and led his men to storm St Lucia's Morne Fortunée, where they tore down the tattered tricolour and flew the king's colours. The boy who had got into debt and fled Geneva without his father's permission was now a respected soldier, singled out for praise in dispatches.

Edward hoped that surely now the king would be proud of him and that his reward would be deployment to the continent, where he could continue his triumphs. Though George was certainly impressed by Edward's military prowess, his reward wasn't a posting to Europe, but a trip to Nova Scotia, where he would be commander of the forces. Though it might not have been what he was hoping for, it was another step up the ladder and as the Prince of Wales languished in London, watching his brothers live out his own military dreams, Edward continued to flourish.

Edward was received in Halifax by Governor John Wentworth and his wife[19], Frances. The Wentworths knew all about reversals of fortune, having once been the glittering first family of New Hampshire. Forced to flee when the American Revolution swept the land, they had no choice but to abandon all their worldly goods in the rush to leave. Five years of exile and judicious networking in England passed before Wentworth was sent to Nova Scotia, where he became governor in 1792, the same year in which Prince Edward was appointed grand master of the Freemasons of Lower Canada. In fact, whilst her husband was enjoying professional success, Frances was building her social circle as ably as she ever did. She had become a very close confidante of Edward's brother, William, when he visited Canada. Now she would add Edward to her increasingly glittering address book too.

Halifax gave Edward both a challenge and a purpose. On his arrival in the harbour he could see that it was desperately in need of improvement. Edward was greeted by an intrigued populace, glad to see the arrival of a British fleet ahead of the French ships that they so feared might be about to descend. The area was depressed, and the presence of a British prince could only spell the start of a new period of prosperity, or so they hoped. For the Royal Navy, a base of operations in Nova Scotia would prove invaluable and as this 1791 survey reveals, improving the woeful defences there was paramount.

'[Among the defences of Halifax] there is not a substantial work, or one that could be brought into use upon any permanent plan of fortifying, though more money has been expended here than would have built a respectable fortress. [Except] the block houses, all the works are composed of sods or fascines, which will scarcely stand in this climate the heavy rains and the frosts of one winter, but as these works were thrown up during the war, and when danger threatened, the most expeditious mode was of course adopted.

[...]

At Halifax there is only one stone magazine [...] that is so old and
so much out of repair as to be in danger of falling. It is not enclosed
in any work, but stands between the town and the Citadel Hill,
exposed to every sort of danger.'[20]

Under Edward's command, all of that would change. With Julie still
in London, he devoted himself to his military duties and to making
the best of life in this distant outpost. When his lover joined him in
Halifax, the couple lost no time in telling the Wentworths how much
they loved the governor's residence and Wentworth, looking to curry
some favour, handed the keys to Edward and literally gave him his home.
The couple set about remodelling the so-called *Friar Lawrence's Cell* to
their own specifications, including a heart-shaped pond which Edward
commissioned for his lover.

As the years passed, Edward oversaw his pet project to overhaul the
defences and military capabilities of Nova Scotia. The woeful structures
that had greeted him on his arrival were gradually replaced by solid,
formidable defences that would be a match for any invading fleet. Just
as he strengthened the lines, so too did he continue to exert his by now
infamous discipline on his garrison, which was as uninspiring as the place
they inhabited. He intended to set an example to his fellow officers and
be dedicated, by-the-book and unswerving. Though he still hoped for
a place in the heart of the European action, Edward knew that this was
unlikely to happen. Instead he made the best of his situation and when
the Duke of York was appointed commander-in-chief, Edward no doubt
had similar hopes for himself. They would remain frustrated.

It was a period of domestic harmony in the life of Edward but as
each winter drew in, his thoughts returned to Great Britain. Ever since
his trip to Germany, cold weather had brought on attacks of agonising
rheumatism and in Halifax, where the winters were bitter, it was worse
than ever. Having endured 'thirteen years absence from home, in this
dreary and distant spot,' Edward was beginning to feel forgotten. He
wrote to his brothers and his parents bemoaning the damage the climate
was doing to his health and begging for a recall to England. Having left
in his teens, he was now 30 and a boy no longer. The time to stop treating
him like one was long overdue.

Coming Home

In early August 1798, Prince Edward took his horse out for a ride in the glorious Canadian summer. He was crossing a bridge when it gave way beneath him and pitched him into a ditch, where his horse rolled on top of him and crushed his leg. By some miracle, Edward escaped with no broken bones, but he was badly shaken and bruised. The bruises would heal, but the injury aggravated Edward's rheumatism and as the weeks passed and his condition didn't improve, he began to realise that the accident might be more fortuitous than it had first appeared. He was suffering in Nova Scotia as it was and with this new injury, his agony was bound to increase. Should the rheumatism be allowed to worsen thanks to the accident, the long-term consequences might be catastrophic.

Edward wrote to his father to seek permission to leave Canada before the weather worsened. He expressed a desire to consult the royal physicians back home and in Halifax, officials were quick to agree. The last thing they wanted was for the prince to sicken or, God forbid, die whilst under their care. Far better to send him home and let the royal doctors take responsibility for his welfare. Fearful that George might accuse him of swinging the lead, Edward even secured a certificate from Dr John Mervin Nooth, Inspector-General of Hospitals in Canada. The certificate confirmed that the injury was so severe that only the spa waters of Bath could possibly treat it. Edward wasn't willing to wait either. That September he told the Prince of Wales that 'I may be obliged at the end of this month or the beginning of the next to embark for England without waiting for [the king's] sanction.'

And let's not forget, he had previous form for leaving a posting without receiving permission to do so.

At home, the king considered his son's request. Edward had been away for well over a decade and in that time the royal household had seen its fair share of scandals and upheaval. There had been a Regency crisis, secret marriages, wars, separation and repeated bouts of illness across the family. Edward had missed all of this and more. He had escaped the bad influence of his brothers and had, George hoped, finally left his tearaway youth behind him to become a useful member of society. He had a fastidious love of details and routine and, just like his father, favoured very specific ways of doing things that rarely, if ever, changed.

'His regularity and method are so uncommon in a young man at his time of life, that they merit attention. He invariably rises before day-light, both in summer and winter, and this has always been his constant practice. The instant he is up he drinks coffee, which is prepared for him over night; when the hair-dresser of his regiment then comes to dress him the first of any Officer; this prevents all murmuring in others being obliged to dress, and be in the field at an early hour. – And, it is a rule with him, that when any thing which may be deemed an inconvenience is necessary to be done, always to set the example.

[…]

He is strict in discipline; but being perfectly impartial, and extremely attentive to the real welfare of the soldier, and generous to all their families when in want, he retains the Affection of the Army.

His regiment he has brought to a degree of perfection, in point of discipline and appearance, seldom equalled in any service.'[21]

With Julie's steadying presence, Edward had apparently grown into the model royal son. Professional, dedicated, loyal and relatively well-disciplined when it came to alcohol and the other vices that his brothers so adored, there was little else that Edward could do to prove that he had finally made up for his past indiscretions.

There was always a risk that Edward might revert to his old ways if he was allowed back into the company of his brothers and the worst that high society had to offer. Should he stay in Canada though, there was a risk of permanent debilitation and in the long eighteenth century, even a seemingly innocuous wound could lead to the worst sort of complications. Nooth's medical findings sealed the deal and the king gave his son the nod. Edward was finally coming home, his lover at his side on the deck on *La Topaze* as they watched the Canadian shore disappear over the horizon.

The boat landed at Spithead on 13 November and Edward came ashore the following day to be greeted by the great and good of Portsmouth.

We can be sure that when Edward accepted their welcome home, he was entirely genuine. As he hastened to Windsor at the invitation of the Prince of Wales, church bells sounded along the route, heralding the return of the prince who had been so long absent. His leg had improved a little during the journey, but he was still unwell, and the limb was weak and badly swollen. The fall from the horse might have been painful, but there's no doubting that it was hugely fortuitous. How he must have blessed that weak little bridge.

Though his last meeting with the king had been an unhappy one, this time, Edward found that he was welcomed with open arms. He never did go to Bath in the end, but instead enjoyed the glittering society of London, repairing each evening to his rooms at Kensington Palace and later Kent House, the home he purchased in Knightsbridge. The protocol-obsessed king and queen tolerated Julie's presence though they certainly had no wish to meet her and Edward knew better than to ask if she could join him in Kensington Palace. Instead he installed her in a stunning house in Brompton and here the hostess of the moment met Edward's brothers and made her mark on London society. Edward spent a large portion of his trip to England trying to convince his father to give him a £4,000 allowance for candles, fuel and other necessities. His brothers received such an allowance, he complained, and life in London was proving worryingly expensive, especially with a provision for Julie being deducted from his income too.

In fact, Edward's stay in England was briefer than he might have hoped. In 1799, he achieved two personal milestones. The first came in April, when he was created Duke of Kent and Strathearn, rare evidence of the approval he sought from his father. This title brought with it a much-needed payment of £12,000. Three weeks later, he was appointed commander-in-chief of the British forces in North America, though this would prove to be a short-lived and ill-fated office. This promotion confirmed that there would never be a place for him in the continental campaign. It also meant a return to his old stomping ground of Nova Scotia, whether he liked it or not. This time the goodbyes were as emotional as they had been perfunctory a few years earlier and for the new Duke of Kent, the parting was made that much more difficult by the fact that he had fought for so long to come home.

The journey back to Nova Scotia took 43 arduous days and though he was welcomed like a returning hero, it was one of the last places on earth that Edward wanted to be. He hoped that a command position might be secured for him at home, perhaps in Scotland. He had one eye on the Master-Generalship of the Ordnance and another on the office of Lord Lieutenant of Ireland, but none of these dreams would come to anything. Instead, Edward was already in Halifax when he learned that his continued loyalty to Julie would prove to be costly. She was, let us not forget, French, and this wasn't a time to be seen cosying up to a Frenchwoman. The Duke of York, commander-in-chief in Britain, told Edward that he could never hope to hold high office in his homeland thanks to her constant presence at his side during his short-lived stopover in England. What one could get away with in Canada, many thousands of miles from home, one couldn't possibly expect to go unremarked in Great Britain.

Edward was stunned. He wrote a long letter to his brother in which he painstakingly detailed the reasons that this was unfair. He and Julie had not lived together in England, nor had they appeared in public together and they'd certainly done nothing to cause a scandal. When Frederick told him that 'such things might be done abroad, but I might depend they could not at home,' Edward shot back that he had heard no gossip about Julie at all, let alone seen 'even in the most scurrilous public prints the shaft of satire [being] levelled at either her or me." Despite Edward's promises that he would install Julie in her own residence and avoid all public appearances with her in the future should he receive his command in the United Kingdom, the outcome didn't change.

So it was that Edward faced the stark truth of his situation. He had soared to the limits of what he could expect to achieve and for now at least he must learn to be content with his lot and reflect that it could be worse. After all, he could be back in Gibraltar.

Back to Gibraltar

After London, Nova Scotia seemed drearier than ever, but this time his stay would be short. In 1800 Edward was back in England, still lame in his injured leg but glad to be in a more temperate climate. He arrived just as the king fell ill and proved to be an attentive son, bridging the gap between the monarch and the Prince of Wales that had widened into a chasm during the long years of Edward's travels. Perhaps still mindful of the gossip Frederick claimed was responsible for Edward's lack of promotion within the United Kingdom, Julie continued to live in her own residence, though she was Edward's social hostess whenever required. It was an arrangement that suited everyone for now.

Having said goodbye to Canada, Edward now bid farewell to his old regiment too. He left the Royal Fusiliers and became a colonel of the Royals (1st Regiment of Foot) instead. Though he mourned the loss of the soldiers to whom he had devoted so many years, Edward took the new appointment as 'proof of [the King's] having condescended to approve of my past conduct in the line of my profession.' He bristled with pride even as he admitted to Frederick that saying goodbye to his old regiment 'almost broke my heart.' No doubt his heart blanched at the thought of a return to the Rock too. On the other hand, since he had been saddled with the task of organising the finances of the estranged Princess of Wales, perhaps Gibraltar was the lesser of two evils.

'His Majesty has been pleased to appoint General his Royal Highness EDWARD Duke of KENT, K.G. to be Governor of Gibraltar.'[22]

With his appointment as Governor of Gibraltar in 1802, in some ways, the Duke of Kent had come full circle. There exists in his correspondence a tantalising hint of a rift between Edward and his brother, Frederick regarding his new position. For some reason – probably financial – it appears that Edward requested a short postponement in moving to Gibraltar. When Frederick said no, it wasn't the friendly tone of a brother, but a definite case of pulling rank. Frederick, it seemed, had been as helpful as he was willing to be for now and politely declined Edward's suggestion, whilst hinting that he shouldn't ask again, but should prepare to sail instead. 'A friendly hint from me,' Frederick told Edward in his letter, 'ought to have been considered by you as only a more delicate way of conveying an order.' When Edward pressed for an audience with their father, Frederick was unequivocal. '[No] paultry [sic] private inconvenience," he told his brother furiously, would be considered "an excuse to procrastinate your stay in this country.'

Over the years, things would get frostier still.

Frederick was devoted to duty and upholding his family honour and he wouldn't let his brother compromise his high standards, so Edward had no choice but to sail. Mercifully, he crossed a sea that was at peace thanks to the Treaty of Amiens. This put a temporary end to Anglo-French hostilities and meant that Edward would be able to devote himself thoroughly to reshaping the Gibraltar garrison without any worry of impending danger. Little did he know that this time, the conflict would come from his own ranks.

General Charles O'Hara had been Governor of Gibraltar since 1795 and his career on the Rock ended only with his death in 1802. During O'Hara's tenure, discipline in the garrison had slumped to an all-time low and with dozens of pubs available to the soldiers, it was slumping further with every passing day. When O'Hara died, the Duke of York knew that his successor must be a man with an eye for detail and a taste for discipline. That man was his brother, Edward, Duke of Kent, but when Frederick advised Edward that 'It will be necessary to establish a due degree of discipline among the troops [which] you will be able to gradually accomplish by a moderate exercise of the power vested in you,' he little knew what the future would hold.

Edward would bring all that he had learned in Germany to bear on his new posting. He had brought the garrison at Gibraltar into line a decade earlier and he was certain that he could do it again. Met with the sight of slovenly, ill-drilled men with little interest in or respect for their station, he was ready to get to work.

Under Edward's regime, slovenliness was to be a thing of the past. The guns sounded to wake the men at 3.30 am and from the moment they rose to the time they went to bed, there was little time to misbehave. Every parade, every drill, every activity was scheduled to ensure that there was no spare time for bad behaviour. Mindful that his men liked to slink off to the pub every evening, Edward introduced a new parade each night to ensure that they couldn't hit the bars too hard. Fastidious in his own habits and appearance, the duke brought his infamous discipline to bear on the outward appearance of his troops as well as their day-to-day regimes. Uniforms were to be tidy, facial hair removed and hair neat. If standards slipped, the miscreants were flogged back into line, but things had been so bad at Gibraltar for so long that Edward's new regime hit the men like a tornado. And with it, there came fallout.

The soldiers would put up with a lot, but when Edward began closing down pubs at a rate of knots, he had crossed the line. In fact, that decision was one that had a detrimental impact on Edward himself, as the governor's income was partially derived from selling alcohol licenses. For *this* governor though, discipline was more important than cash. Don't forget that Edward had already put down a small mutiny in Canada and in Gibraltar, history was about to repeat itself. Though he didn't know it, as 1802 drew to an end, mutineers were conspiring in the garrison to overthrow what they regarded as a tyrannical regime. They 'had been used worse than Slaves,' they declared, 'and would no longer bear it.'

On Christmas Eve, the Royals had received their pay and had spent the day drinking. They returned to the garrison in a mind to mutiny and appealed to the men of the 25th and 54th Foot to join them. However, the latter two regiments had yet to be paid so, sober and with empty purses, they declined the invitation. The booze-fuelled Royals marched to the prince's quarters and called for him to come out. Instead they were addressed by General Charles Barnett, who urged them to return to their barracks. When they refused, the mutineers were met by the soldiers of the 54th Foot, who were determined to protect the governor – at least until payday. As they opened fire, the mutineers fled. Under the protection of darkness and chaos, Edward was unable to establish exactly who had led the mutiny against him and Barnett, perhaps feeling a little of the Christmas spirit, suggested that Edward should show mercy on this occasion. Suffering once more from rheumatism, Edward nevertheless addressed the garrison and warned them that any repeat of the events of Christmas Eve would be met with the sternest possible punishment.

We may wonder at the motives of General Barnett too. Apparently, a peacemaker, he had acted as caretaker Governor of Gibraltar in the months between General O'Hara's death and Edward's arrival and he was subject to the duke's strict discipline just like everyone else. One old soldier who had lived through the mutiny told Edward's early biographer, Erskine Neale, that Barnett rubbed his hands with glee at the outbreak of mutiny. 'It was the best thing that could have happened,' Barnett told a fellow officer. 'Now we shall get rid of him.'[23]

That repeat came within a matter of days. By now the 25th Foot had been paid and the men had done some drinking of their own. They turned to the Royals and said that, if the mutiny was still on, they wanted to be part of it. This time it was the Royals who declined, so the 25th Foot marched out in search of Edward and met, just as the Royals had, the 54th Foot. It was the start of days of mutiny with each fiercely put down only to rise up again the next day. Through all of it Edward had held back, belying his tyrannical reputation, but as 1803 dawned he had had enough.

The mutineers had been given a free pass on Christmas Eve but when increasingly violent unrest continued into New Year's Eve, Edward ordered the arrest of the mutineers of the 25th Foot. Although the *Morning Post* declared that the riots could not be ascribed to 'the conduct of the Duke of KENT, as the authors and abettors of that system whisper,'[24] they were wrong. The mutiny had come about precisely as a consequence of the sudden change in the circumstances of the garrison, as men who had grown used to a slapdash regime were met with a whirlwind of stern and unbending discipline. Though Frederick had encouraged 'a moderate exercise' of power, moderate was relative when it came to the rule-loving Edward. Instead, he had gone in all guns blazing.

The court martial of a dozen mutineers was over in a couple of days. Ten of them were sentenced to death; Edward commuted seven of those sentences to transportation, but an unlucky trio faced a firing squad made up of their former comrades. The two mutineers who had not been sentenced to death or transportation were handed 1,000 lashes each, sentences that were later repealed. On the day that the sentences were doled out, Edward wrote to the Prince of Wales and poured out his feelings on the '*slavery* I have submitted to, to forward the service.' Though the thought of remaining in Gibraltar, with all the memories it now carried, was abhorrent to him, the idea of leaving was even worse. '*Honor* [sic] forbids me,' he wrote.

'It is my firm resolution to remain till I can deliver my trust up into the hands of some abler and more *popular* man than myself, in a state in which I can say to him, 'You will receive the garrison of Gibraltar in a state of order that will not discredit the king's service. In affecting this I have gone thro' the severest trial man *could* experience. [Once I] quit this, it will be with the firm and decided intention of never seeing it again.'[25]

Determined to stay he might have been, but Edward was equally determined that he would decide when to leave too. His decision to remain wasn't stubbornness but an attempt by a man whose authority had taken a serious knock to wrest back control and save face. In truth, he didn't want to remain on the Rock at all, but nor was he willing to turn tail and flee until he had stayed long enough to make it clear that the mutiny was not why he was running away. Edward asked the Prince of Wales and the Duke of York to ensure that he could leave Gibraltar on account of his health no later than early May. Edward then wrote his own account of the events of the mutiny to the Duke of York, laying the blame firmly at the feet of the surly and indolent soldiers he had found on the Rock.

'[Scarcely] a day passed that men were not confined from off guards for drunkenness or sleeping on their posts, for acts of insubordination, and for crimes committed upon the property and persons of the inhabitants. Punishments of course unavoidably became necessary, and the repetition of it frequent. Still the evil did not decrease, and I then felt that my whole attention ought to be devoted to form a system for conducting the several duties both public and regimental, founded upon the principle of keeping the soldier constantly employed, and thus by depriving him of the opportunities of committing crimes, prevent the frequent reoccurrence of them. How far I succeeded in this object your Royal Highness will best be able to judge when I inform you that since it has been inforced [sic], the commission of crimes and the consequent punishments have been reduced by more than one half.'[26]

Edward went on to claim that the roots of the mutiny lay in the lax discipline that General O'Hara had allowed, which had created 'a set of men who were inferior in every respect to the worse militia regiment

I had ever met with.'[27] So dire was the situation with the Royals that he made them his personal project. Had officers wholly supported his new regime, Edward believed that things would have been very different indeed. It was a combination of long-held bad habits and drink that had come together to cause catastrophe, he concluded. Neither he nor Barnett had any inkling of mutinous feelings, said the Duke of Kent, and if they had, the mutiny would've been quashed before it could begin.

When Edward was unexpectedly summoned back to England by his father, his agitation grew. At Gibraltar he had experienced a situation unlike any he had ever known before and he feared exactly what might be waiting for him when he reached home. 'My character as a soldier and as a man, is at *stake*,' he told the Prince of Wales. 'Never have I experienced a trial like the present one.'[28]

Fallout

The mutiny in Gibraltar had hit the headlines and with it, the search was on for someone to blame. The executed mutineers had been Dutch and Irish, and some pointed the finger at their countrymen, as though their presence alone was all the explanation that was needed. Some railed against the culture of drunken debauchery on the Rock and applauded the prince's hardline efforts to bring it under control, whilst others theorised that the responsibility could only rest with the Duke of Kent himself. Edward believed differently, for when he left Gibraltar, he was convinced that the garrison was more disciplined and peaceful than it had ever been before. Perhaps it was, because the men were as pleased to hear that he was leaving as they had been annoyed at his arrival.

Edward's office was not revoked when he arrived in England. In fact, he was still officially Governor of Gibraltar until the day he died, but to all intents and purposes, he was replaced in the post by Major General Sir Thomas Trigge following his recall. The duke arrived back in England in May, having handed Trigge his self-penned *Code of Standing Orders*, which sought to govern in minute detail every movement made by the soldiers. Trigge was astonished not only by the work that Edward had put into his pet project, but also by how restrictive the 300-page book was. Although he initially attempted to put the code into practice, before

Trigge had been in charge for a month, he had completely abandoned his predecessor's manual.

Edward took his recall as a personal insult. Determined to clear his name, he requested an enquiry as a 'means of vindicating my character, which as an officer I cannot but feel stands at this moment under a stigma in the eyes of my profession'[29]. Having been so determined to manage his own departure from Gibraltar, the fact that he had been recalled sent a message about his conduct that shook the duke. Edward had spent the better part of his life in the service of his father and his country and he was determined to clear his name quickly enough to play his part in the renewed hostilities against France. With the Prince of Wales on his side, he was sure he would soon be back in the saddle.

Wales took Edward's case to the prime minister, Henry Addington. From the tone and content of his letter, it's clear that he fully agreed with Edward's belief that his treatment had been outrageous.

'You send a man out to control a garrison all but in a state of open mutiny. You tell him to terminate such a disgraceful state of things. You assure him of the unqualified support of Government in his undertaking. He goes out. He finds matters infinitely worse than they were represented. The impending outbreak occurs. He quells it thoroughly. By way of reward you disgrace him! If you want to deter an officer from doing his duty or desire to encourage a mutinous soldier your tactics are admirable. They cannot fail to attain such a result. Edward may well complain. He were neither officer nor man, if he were silent.'[30]

Neither Edward nor George's outraged representations made a difference to the fate of the Governor of Gibraltar. Frederick agreed to meet Edward face to face and told him that there would be no inquiry, though Frederick agreed to censure Trigge for throwing out the prince's lovingly crafted code of conduct. He warned Edward darkly that he intended to speak to their father and, Edward assumed, confirm that he would not be returning to Gibraltar. Lest there be any doubt, Frederick left his brother in no doubt that he held him entirely responsible for the mutiny. 'He condemned my conduct from first to last as marked by cruelty and oppression,' Edward told a friend. For a man who believed in honour and duty so strongly, it was a shattering blow.

Worse was yet to come when the king, who Edward had always longed to please, joined Frederick in pointing the finger of blame at him. George III was 'persuaded that the circumstances which produc'd [Edward's] removal from Gibraltar may be attributed to over-zeal on his part,'[31] and for his son, there could be no worse a conclusion. As Edward told the Prince of Wales, 'My heart is quite broke', for he knew that this effectively meant the end of what could and should have been a glittering career. It was the end of discipline in Gibraltar too. With the hardline governor gone, the garrison slipped swiftly back into its old vices.

There remains one final twist in this tale. Recall if you will Mary Anne Clarke, the mistress who sold military commissions under the apparently unsuspecting nose of her lover, the Duke of York. When she faced Parliament in 1810 and told of conspiracy and corruption, one of the people she accused of misconduct was none other than Prince Edward, Duke of Kent. Edward had supposedly been so incensed at Frederick's behaviour towards him after the mutiny that he had nursed a seething hatred for his brother through the years, plotting his revenge until the moment was right. If Mary was to be believed, that moment came in 1808.

Mary claimed that Edward's secretary, Thomas Dodd, told her that if Frederick were to lose his position, then he would be replaced by a much more deserving man – who else but the Duke of Kent? Somehow the duke and Dodd had learned of Mary's sideline in selling commissions and they offered her thousands of pounds if she agreed to testify against Frederick and bring him down. Mary was quick to add that she had never received the promised payment.

It's here that things take a rather confusing turn. It wasn't Frederick's apparent lack of support that had offended Edward, it seemed, but quite the opposite. According to Mary, Frederick had intervened to prevent Edward facing a court martial that would have inevitably found against him.

'I believe there is scarcely a military man in the kingdom, who was at
Gibraltar during the duke of Kent's command of that fortress, but

is satisfied that the duke [sic] of York's refusal of a Court Martial to his Royal brother, *afforded an incontestible* [sic] *proof* of his *regard* for the *military character*, and honor of the duke of Kent; for if a Court Martial had been granted to the governor of Gibraltar, I always understood there was but one opinion, as to what would have been *the result*; and then, the duke of Kent would have lost several thousands a year, and incurred such public reflections, that would, most probably, have been painful to his *honorable* and *acute* feelings. It was, however, this *act of affection* for the duke of Kent, that laid the foundation of that hatred which has followed the Commander in Chief up to the present moment; - and to this *unnatural feeling*, he is solely indebted for all the misfortunes and disgrace to which he has been introduced.'[32]

The very idea of it is as absurd as it is melodramatic. Though Edward received a promotion to field marshal in 1805, there was no way on earth that he would have been made commander-in-chief of the British army in Frederick's place. A long-nurtured revenge plot such as this one doesn't feel like Edward's style at all. He wasn't a man who kept his own counsel, but rather an inveterate letter writer who liked to make his opinions known. By 1808 he could be in no doubt that his influence in the army was long since over and whatever else Edward was, he wasn't a fantasist. He would have been well aware that the role of commander-in-chief would never be his, short of a miracle occurring. In the court of George III, miracles were in short supply.

To Europe

When it came to Gibraltar, there was nothing Edward could do but accept his fate. It was a stain on his reputation that he felt keenly but, with his father's health in decline and the Duke of York no longer willing to enter into further discussion, he had been forced into a professional cul-de-sac. With no other choice, Edward settled into a domestic life with Julie, this time at Castle Hill Lodge in Ealing. The lodge had previously been owned by none other than Maria Fitzherbert, the secret bride of the Prince of Wales. Although Edward was still technically the Governor of Gibraltar and occasionally made a little hint about the enquiry he had been denied or his wish to somehow serve his country, from the Duke of York, the ailing king and the government alike, the answer was always silence. Not a *no*, just not anything at all.

Instead Edward followed the path taken by so many other genteel but directionless fellows and occupied his time with charitable pursuits. He was appointed Ranger of Hampton Court Park in September 1805 and as the years passed, the sting of his removal from Gibraltar was salved. As George III's health collapsed, Edward became a familiar sight at Windsor, but he never allowed himself to get caught up in the feuding between Wales and his parents. Instead he trod the middle ground as a friend to both, and no doubt allowed himself a bitter smile of revenge when Frederick, Duke of York, found his own woes splashed across the headlines. His own supposed part in the scandal received little notice. Instead, the fallout from Mary Anne Clarke's scandalous adventures landed firmly on the head of the Duke of York and eventually cost him the job he loved.

To all intents and purposes, the Duke of Kent was living in something approaching a very busy retirement. He visited his sickening father and dying sister, Amelia, paid court to the Prince of Wales when he was appointed Prince Regent and passed gentle hours with his mother, Queen Charlotte. Yet Edward wasn't willing to go quietly and with his elder brother's new rank came a renewed wave of appeals for a return to active duty. George had been happy to support Edward's appeals in the past but now he was Regent and had the power to make Edward's dream come true, he did no such thing. Edward believed that Prinny would grant him the Ordnance as a consolation prize for all that he had lost but instead George maintained the status quo. Prince Edward remained out of a job.

This was the start of an unhappy period for the two brothers. The Prince Regent was embroiled in an ongoing feud with his daughter, Charlotte, which even caused her to run away from home on one occasion. Edward, however, was a supporter of the young lady, perhaps seeing in her a shadow of his former self, desperately appealing to his father for approval that he would never receive.

Edward became something of a father figure to Charlotte and was a constant support when she fought with Prinny for the right to marry Leopold of Saxe-Coburg-Saalfeld. When that dream came true for the young princess in 1816, Charlotte and her new husband tentatively suggested that Edward might be ready for a marriage of his own, and they had just the candidate in mind. She was Princess Victoria of Saxe-Coburg-Saalfeld, a widow since the death of her husband, Emich Carl, 2nd Prince of Leiningen, in 1814.

Born to Franz Frederick Anton, Duke of Saxe-Coburg-Saalfeld, and Countess Augusta of Reuss-Ebersdorf, Victoria had enjoyed a privileged upbringing. Bright, charming and attractive, she was the mother of two children by her late husband and had served as the Regent of Leiningen since her husband's death. Not content with the lot that fate had dealt her, the social-climbing Victoria would not be single for long. The idea of marriage took root somewhere in the back of Edward's mind, slowly germinating.

Edward's finances had been in dire straits from the very start and even now he struggled to balance the books and keep himself in the manner to which he had become accustomed. The purchase of Castle Hill Lodge, which had provided him with a sanctuary, had also provided him with another source of debt and when Napoleon was vanquished, the duke began to wonder whether he and Julie could make a better and more affordable go of it on the continent.

In the height of summer 1815, Julie and Edward left for Paris and a home they had rented. After a brief stopover they travelled on to Brussels and from there, Edward paid a short trip to Russia, where he supposedly discussed the possibility of a marriage to one of the sisters-in-law of Tsar Alexander I. Though nothing came of 'the rumour in these Papers of an intended marriage between the Duke of KENT and the Princess AMELIA of Baden, sister to the Empress of RUSSIA,'[33] Edward did manage to convince the tsar to foot the bill for his trip to Russia. A small victory, but still a victory. Of more significance was the stopover he made for an audience with Victoria, the woman who would eventually become his wife. Edward was plotting.

Just as William had been before him, Edward was aware that he might one day be called upon to further the line of succession. The Prince

Regent had just one child, Charlotte, and none of his siblings had produced a single legitimate heir between them. Charlotte and Leopold continued to sing the praises of Victoria and to Julie's distress, rumours of a courtship appeared in the press. They were swiftly denied, but they were truer than anyone could have guessed.

> 'We are authorised to contradict, positively, the report of the Duke of KENT's marriage with the Princess Dowager of LINANGES, which is totally without foundation.'[34]

Edward was tempted by the thought of the marriage yet after nearly thirty years with Julie as his consort, the knowledge of the pain it would cause her was acute. On the other hand, the certainty that a marriage would bring in a handsome payment from Parliament couldn't be so easily set aside and the more the prince considered his echoing coffers, the more he began to think about the future. Secretly, with not a word to Julie, Edward began to make enquiries about the eligible Victoria.

Husband and Father

There's no doubting that Edward loved Julie and that the prospect of leaving her was one that he didn't approach lightly. Yet, like his brothers, he had a selfish streak that together with his love of spending, made for a fatal combination. He might have hoped for delicacy, but his secret investigations into the possibility of a marriage to Victoria took on a new urgency with the death of Princess Charlotte and her newborn child. Suddenly the line of succession had been cut off at its roots and the royal brothers needed to get married and start producing heirs and spares as quickly as they could. With the death of Charlotte, Julie would certainly have feared for her own relationship, and the rumours of the prince's interest in Victoria couldn't possibly have escaped her.

Edward secured the agreement of his prospective bride in 1818, but he had a condition for the marriage. He would only set Julie aside on the understanding that he had 'the means given me to render my old & faithful friend [Julie] independent & comfortable *for life*; for without being able to do *that at once*, I never could agree to the sacrifice.' Once he had satisfied himself that she would receive an ongoing allowance,

Edward arranged for a friend to call him back to England on supposedly innocent business. Though he would supposedly only be absent for a couple of months, this would be his excuse to leave Julie once and for all.

When Edward said goodbye to Julie, she saw through the subterfuge immediately. She wept as they parted in Brussels, he bound for London and she for Paris. It was the last time the couple would ever meet. Though some have since theorised that the childless couple may have undergone a secret marriage of their own earlier in their relationship, there is no proof of this. Julie continued to live in Paris in quiet, dignified comfort. It was here that she died in 1830, aged 69.

After twenty-seven years, the affair was over. Edward was to be a husband at last.

'The Message announcing the intended marriage of the Duke of KENT with the Princess Dowager of LEININGEN [was] brought down last night. [...] The Princess herself has an establishment and dower, amounting to between 4 and 5,000l. sterling per annum.'[35]

Along with his fiancée's dowry, Parliament agreed that the prince's marriage was worth an increase in his allowance of £6,000 per year. With that decided, he set off for Coburg and the bride who awaited him. The couple was married at Amorbach Castle on 29 May 1818 and again in that double wedding ceremony at Kew six weeks later. Once they had completed their social engagements, the newlyweds returned to Amorbach, where they remained for several months.

The newly minted Duchess of Kent was quick to do her duty and within weeks of the wedding, she was pregnant. The child would be heir to the British throne and despite Edward's finances being more stretched than ever by his payments to Julie, he knew the importance of Victoria giving birth in Great Britain. The Prince Regent did all he could to obstruct Edward's plans but eventually the Duke of Kent won through and with a fat loan from a couple of noble friends, Edward and Victoria set off for England.

'THIS morning, at a quarter past four o'clock, the Duchess of Kent was happily delivered of a Princess. Her Royal Highness is, God be praised, as well as can be expected, and the young Princess is in perfect health.'[36]

The Duke and Duchess of Kent only had one child, but she was to become a royal legend. Their daughter was born on 24 May 1819 and was named Alexandrina Victoria. When Edward's old friend, Dr John Fisher, heard of the birth he commented, 'May the little princess resemble her father in character, but not in destiny', and his wish was certainly granted. Little Victoria would never experience the financial embarrassment that her father had endured, nor his search for a meaningful role. She was to become one of the most famous and powerful queens that the world had ever known.

Edward adored his little daughter and relished the part he had played in preserving the future of his line. He proudly told visitors to Kensington Palace as they gazed at the baby in her crib that they were looking at the girl who would one day be queen. Yet still Edward's finances were as shaky as ever and he rented Woolbrook Cottage in Sidmouth, hoping that a break from London might save the family some much-needed cash. It was a fateful decision.

The Fatal Boots

It was on the road to Sidmouth that Edward stopped off in Salisbury to visit Fisher, by now the Bishop there. The weather was perilous, and Edward was caught in a storm. Freezing cold and drenched to his skin, he declined to change out of his wet boots and as a result contracted a cold which sent him to bed when he reached Sidmouth. The press was sure that a man like Edward, physically imposing, robust and well-used to difficult conditions, would soon recover, but they were to be fatally mistaken.

The duchess summoned George III's physician, Sir David Dundas, to come and treat her husband. Already fully occupied with caring for the king, Dundas was unable to leave his patient and instead suggested his colleague, William Maton. Maton hastened to Sidmouth and began a programme of intensive treatment aimed at combatting the fever that had seized the duke.

Edward knew that his end was near. He spent his last days putting his affairs in order and used what remained of his strength to put his signature to his last will and testament.

'This morning the melancholy tidings of the death of the Duke of KENT arrived at the Palace, to the great grief of everyone who had the honour and pleasure of knowing his Royal Highness.'[37]

The man who had survived mutiny, shame and scandal died on 23 January 1820. Six days later his father, George III, followed him to the grave. As the king lay in state, Edward was buried at Windsor in a vast coffin of more than seven feet in length. His only child[38] would one day give her name to an era. Through the long years of her legendary reign, Queen Victoria adored the father she had barely known.

Afterword

And so, we reach the end of our jaunt through the lives of the eldest sons of George III and Charlotte of Mecklenburg-Strelitz. They were kings, princes, and dukes, each boy growing into a man in the long shadow of their father. As the sons of a king who faced demons of his own, it's not surprising that these men battled to carve out a place in a world that expected them to follow the example set by their pious parents. They rarely succeeded, and in their scandals and struggles we see the humans behind the titles and grandeur, as fallible as any other men.

Their challenges might have been different to those faced by their sisters, but the royal brothers lived lives that were far from the cossetted, privileged ideals we might have expected. Instead they trod a thin line between duty and ambition, striving to become their own men in the blaze of the spotlight.

Today we remember them as *Prinny* and the *Grand Old Duke*, or even the *Sailor King* and the *Father of the Canadian Crown*. For better or worse, each brother made his mark and their lives tell the story of a changing world, of expanding horizons and regal ambitions. King George III was not an easy act to follow, but it didn't stop his sons from trying.

Notes

Introduction
1. Georgian Papers Online (http://gpp.rct.uk, October 2019) RA GEO/MAIN/16518, George III to Prince William, 8 September 1785.

Act One
1. Georgian Papers Online (http://gpp.rct.uk, October 2019) RA GEO/ADD/4/204/2, George III to Prince William, 13 June, 1779.
2. Georgian Papers Online (http://gpp.rct.uk, October 2019) RA GEO/MAIN/54227-54232, Frederick, Prince of Wales, to his son George, 13 January 1749.
3. *London Evening Post* (London, England), 10 August 1762–12 August 1762; issue 5422.
4. Georgian Papers Online (http://gpp.rct.uk, October 2019) RA GEO/MAIN/36345-36347, Queen Charlotte to George, Prince of Wales, 12 August 1770.
5. Hibbert, Christopher (1976). *George IV*. London: Penguin Books, p. 24.
6. Georgian Papers Online (http://gpp.rct.uk, October 2019) RA GEO/MAIN/36345-36347, Queen Charlotte to George, Prince of Wales, 12 August 1770.

Act Two
1. *Gazetteer and London Daily Advertiser* (London, England), Friday, 13 August, 1762; issue 10392.
2. *Whitehall Evening Post (1770)* (London, England). 12 October 1780–14 October 1780.
3. *The Salisbury and Winchester Journal* (Salisbury, England), Monday, 18 February 1788; issue 2593.
4. Georgian Papers Online (http://gpp.rct.uk, October 2019) RA GEO/MAIN/44700, Prince William to George, Prince of Wales, 10 February 1786.
5. *The Times* (London, England). Saturday, 24 January 1789; issue 1230.
6. *The Reading Mercury and Oxford Gazette, etc* (Reading, England). Monday, 26 January 1789; issue 1410.
7. Georgian Papers Online (http://gpp.rct.uk, November 2019) RA GEO/MAIN/38396, Speech of George, Prince of Wales, c.30 January 1789.

8. *The Times* (London, England), Wednesday, 3 December 1788, issue 1187.

9. *The Telegraph* (London, England), Tuesday, 30 December 1794, issue 1.

10. Georgian Papers Online (http://gpp.rct.uk, October 2019) RA GEO/ MAIN/39076-39077, George III to George, Prince of Wales, 8 April 1795.

11. Aspinall, Arthur (ed.) (1963). *The Correspondence of George, Prince of Wales, Vol II*. London: Cassell, p.64.

12. *The Telegraph* (London, England), Tuesday, 30 December 1794, issue 1.

13. Bury, Lady Charlotte (1839). *Diary Illustrative of the Times of George the Fourth, Vol. I*. London: Henry Colburn, pp.38-39.

14. Robins, Jane (2006), *The Trial of Queen Caroline: The Scandalous Affair that Nearly Ended a Monarchy*. New York: Simon and Schuster, pp.17–8.

15. Ibid.

16. *The Times* (London, England), Saturday, 9 January 1796; issue 3487.

17. Georgian Papers Online (http://gpp.rct.uk, October 2019) RA GEO/ MAIN/39169-39174, George, Prince of Wales, to Caroline, Princess of Wales, 21 April 1796.

18. *Morning Post* (London, England). Saturday, 11 October 1806; issue 11124.

19. *Lancaster Gazetter* (Lancaster, England), Saturday, 16 February 1811; issue 505.

20. Georgian Papers Online (http://gpp.rct.uk, October 2019) RA GEO/ MAIN/36666, Queen Charlotte to the Prince Regent, 14 December 1813.

21. *The Times* (London, England), Monday, 6 May 1816; issue 9827.

22. *Morning Chronicle* (London, England), Friday, 7 November 1817; issue 15138.

23. *Morning Post* (London, England), Friday, 21 January 1820; issue 15299.

24. *Glasgow Herald* (Glasgow, Scotland). 30 June, 1820; issue 1828.

25. *The Times* (London, England), Wednesday, 7 June 1820; issue 10953.

26. *Morning Post* (London, England), Wednesday, 16 August 1820; issue 15418.

27. Bury, Lady Charlotte Campbell (1838). *The Murdered Queen!*. London: W Emans, p.655.

28. George later tried to convince Parliament to give him the rented diamonds as a gift. They refused.

29. Georgian Papers Online (http://gpp.rct.uk, October 2019) RA GEO/ ADD/3/50, George IV to Sir William Knighton, 14 August 1821.

30. Arbuthnot, Harriet (1950). *The Journal of Mrs Arbuthnot, 1820-1832, Vol I*. London: Macmillan, p108.

31. Anonymous (1938). *The Quarterly Review, Vol. 270*. London: John Murray, p128.

32. *The Examiner* (London, England), Sunday 27 June, 1830; issue 1139.

33. Morison, Stanley (1935). *The History of the Times: The Thunderer in the Making, 1785-1841*. London: The Times (1950), p.268.

Act Three

1. *Gazetteer and London Daily Advertiser* (London, England), Wednesday, August 17 1763; issue 10742.
2. Aspinall, Arthur (1971). *The Correspondence of George, Prince of Wales, Vol I*. Oxford: Oxford University Press, p.79.
3. Letitia Smith married Sir John Lade, 2nd Baronet, and the couple became famed both for their scandalous lifestyle and equestrian skills.
4. Aspinall, Arthur (ed.) (1966). *The Later Correspondence of George III, Vol I*. Cambridge: Cambridge University Press, p.115.
5. Georgian Papers Online (http://gpp.rct.uk, October 2019) RA GEO/ ADD/4/15, Frederick, Duke of York, to Prince William, 4 January 1782.
6. Ibid., p.255.
7. Marsh, Charles (1832). *The Clubs of London: Vol I*. London: Henry Colburn and Richard Bentley, pp.91-92.
8. Aspinall, Arthur (ed.) (1971). *The Correspondence of George, Prince of Wales: Vol I*. Oxford: Oxford University Press, p.417.
9. Minto, Gilbert Elliot, Earl of (1874). *Life and Letters of Sir Gilbert Elliot First Earl of Minto from 1751 to 1806, Vol. I*. London: Longmans, Green, and Company, p.275.
10. Ibid., p.264.
11. *Morning Star* (London, England). Thursday, May 28 1789; issue 91.
12. Aspinall, Arthur (ed.) (1966). *The Later Correspondence of George III, Vol. I*. Cambridge: Cambridge University Press, pp.545-547.
13. Frederick William II would go on to have several further children by way of his multiple bigamous marriages.
14. *London Gazette* (London, England), 27 September 1791–1 October 1791; issue 13347.
15. Georgian Papers Online (http://gpp.rct.uk, October 2019) RA GEO/ MAIN/38623, Lord Malmesbury to George, Prince of Wales, 30 September, 1791.
16. *St. James's Chronicle or the British Evening Post* (London, England), 4 October 1791–6 October 1791; issue 4673.
17. Aspinall, Arthur (ed.) (1962). *The Later Correspondence of George III, Vol. II*. Cambridge: Cambridge University Press, p.67.
18. Georgian Papers Online (http://gpp.rct.uk, October 2019) RA GEO/ MAIN/38944, Frederick, Duke of York and Albany, to George, Prince of Wales, 11 July1794.
19. Aspinall, Arthur (ed.) (1962). *The Later Correspondence of George III, Vol. II*. Cambridge: Cambridge University Press, p.89.
20. Georgian Papers Online (http://gpp.rct.uk, October 2019) RA GEO/ MAIN/38988, Prince Ernest to George, Prince of Wales, 1 December 1794.
21. Georgian Papers Online (http://gpp.rct.uk, October 2019) RA GEO/ MAIN/38985-38987, Henry Dundas to Frederick, Duke of York and Albany, 27 November 1794.

22. Aspinall, Arthur (ed.) (1962). *The Later Correspondence of George III, Vol. III*. Cambridge: Cambridge University Press, p.247.

23. Ibid., p.285.

24. Ibid., p.286.

25. Hogan, Denis (1808). *An Appeal to the Public, and a Farewell Address to the Army*. London: G Gorman, p.56.

26. *Morning Post* (London, England), Friday, February 3 1809; issue 11863.

27. *Northampton Mercury* (Northampton, England), Saturday, 18 March 1809; issue 2.

28. Ibid.

29. Anonymous (1815). *The Parliamentary Debates from the Year 1803 to the Present Time, Volume XXXI*. London: TC Hansard, p.1139.

30. *Morning Chronicle* (London, England), Monday, 7 August 1820; issue 15999.

31. *The Times* (London, England), Monday, 7 August 1820; issue 11005.

32. The building eventually became known as Stafford House for over a century, until it was purchased by Viscount Leverhulme and renamed Lancaster House.

33. Urban, Sylvanus (1827). *The Gentleman's Magazine: and Historical Chronicle, Volume XCVII*. London: John Harris, p.265.

Act Four

1. *Gazetteer and New Daily Advertiser* (London, England), Monday, 26 August 1765; issue 11374.

2. Majendie was initially engaged as an English teacher to Queen Charlotte. He became a loyal and long-time member of the royal household.

3. As 1st Viscount Hood, he later rose to the very pinnacle of the Royal Navy, serving as First Naval Lord, among other offices.

4. Georgian Papers Online (http://gpp.rct.uk, October 2019) GEO/ADD/15/0460, Letter from George III to Major General Jacob de Budé, 11 June 1779.

5. Georgian Papers Online (http://gpp.rct.uk, October 2019) RA GEO/ADD/4/204/3, Queen Charlotte to Prince William, 9 July,1779.

6. Georgian Papers Online (http://gpp.rct.uk, October 2019) RA GEO/MAIN/44604-44605, Prince William to George III, 18 October 1779.

7. Georgian Papers Online (http://gpp.rct.uk, October 2019) RA GEO/MAIN/44611-44612, Prince William to George III, 26 January 1780.

8. *Freeman's Journal or The North American Intelligencer* (London, England), Wednesday,23 January 1782; issue 40.

9. Admiral Francois-Joseph-Paul de Grasse-Rouville, comte de Grasse, led the French fleet that prevented the Royal Navy from reinforcing Yorktown. With escape by sea and the hope of British reinforcements denied him, Lord Cornwallis was left with no option but to surrender. It was a decisive moment in the War of Independence.

10. *Freeman's Journal or The North-American Intelligencer* (London, England), Wednesday, 23 January, 1782; issue 40.

11. Aspinall, Arthur (ed.) (1966). *The Later Correspondence of George III, Vol. I.* Cambridge: Cambridge University Press, p.69.

12. Georgian Papers Online (http://gpp.rct.uk, October 2019) RA GEO/ ADD/4/204/39, Queen Charlotte to Prince William, 7 October 1783[?].

13. Ibid.

14. Georgian Papers Online (http://gpp.rct.uk, October 2019) RA GEO/ MAIN/44658-44659, Prince William to George, Prince of Wales, 23 April 1784.

15. Georgian Papers Online (http://gpp.rct.uk, October 2019) RA GEO/ MAIN/44664-44665, Prince William to George, Prince of Wales, 23 July 1784.

16. Georgian Papers Online (http://gpp.rct.uk, October 2019) RA GEO/ MAIN/44713-44714, Prince William to George, Prince of Wales, 1 December 1786.

17. Though some have attributed the nickname *Silly Billy* to William IV, in fact, that dubious honour belongs to his brother-in-law, Prince William Frederick, Duke of Gloucester and Edinburgh.

18. Georgian Papers Online (http://gpp.rct.uk, October 2019) RA GEO/ MAIN/44763-44768, Prince William, to George III, 20 May 1787.

19. This did nothing to dent Schomberg's career and he continued in the Royal Navy until his retirement in 1795. He began a second career, first as a historian and then as a commissioner of the navy, where he remained until his death in 1813.

20. Hamilton, Richard Vesey (ed.) (1903). *Letters and Papers of Admiral of the Fleet Sir Thos. Byam Martin, Vol I.* Navy Records Society: London, p.36.

21. Jeffrey, Reginald (ed.) (1907). *Dyott's Diary 1781-1845: Vol I.* London: Archibald Constable and Company, Ltd, p.37.

22. Georgian Papers Online (http://gpp.rct.uk, October 2019) RA GEO/ MAIN/44806-44807, Prince William to George III, 27 December 1787.

23. Wraxall, Nathaniel (1836). *Posthumous Memoirs of His Own Time, Vol III.* London: Richard Bentley, p.154.

24. Arundel, Throphilus (1880). *Caroline von Linsingen and King William the Fourth.* London: W Swan Sonnenschein & Allen, pp.66-72.

25. Ibid., pp.76-78.

26. Ibid., p.164.

27. Caroline recovered from her brush with death and lived until 1815. Her husband outlived her by well over a decade.

28. Adolphus, John (1839). *Memoirs of John Bannister, Comedian, Vol. I.* London: Richard Bentley, pp.126-127.

29. Boaden, James (1831). *The Life of Mrs Jordan, Vol I.* London: Edward Bull, p.361.

30. *Jordan* was also slang for a chamber pot.
31. She was named Frances.
32. Dorothea was born in 1787 and Lucy in 1789. Dora also had a son in 1788, but he died at birth.
33. *Northampton Mercury* (Northampton, England), Saturday, 22 October 1791; issue 33.
34. *The Times* (London, England). Thursday, October 13 1791; issue 2152.
35. *Morning Post* (London, England). Wednesday, 19 October 1791; issue 5768.
36. *Evening Mail* (London, England). 31 October–2 November 1791; issue 419.
37. *The Times* (London: England). Tuesday, 29 November 1791; issue 2193.
38. They were George, Henry, Sophia, Mary, Frederick, Elizabeth, Adolphus, Augusta, Augustus and Amelia. All lived long lives.
39. Their modern descendants include former prime minister, David Cameron.
40. She married Napoleon's aide-de-camp, Charles Joseph, compte de Flahaut, in 1817 and became a celebrated hostess, living to the ripe old age of 79.
41. Wellesley-Pole was a favourite at the court of George IV, but he was severely lacking in morality. He splashed Catherine's cash in every gambling and bawdy house he could find and even infected her with venereal disease. She got her revenge after her death in 1825, by disinheriting her husband and leaving everything to their eldest son instead.
42. *The Times* (London, England). Thursday, 12 December 1811; issue 8471.
43. Boaden, James (1831). *The Life of Mrs Jordan, Vol II*. London: Edward Bull, pp.273-275.
44. Georgian Papers Online (http://gpp.rct.uk, October 2019) RA GEO/ ADD/4/148, William , Duke of Clarence, to Sophia FitzClarence, undated.
45. *Morning Chronicle* (London, England). Saturday, 20 February 1813; issue 13664.
46. *Hull Packet* (Hull, England). Tuesday, 16 July 1816; issue 1551.
47. In 1817, William also mourned the death of his son, Henry FitzClarence, who died in India in his early twenties.
48. Jerrold, Clare (1914). *The Story of Dorothy Jordan*. London: Eveleigh Nash, p338.
49. *Leeds Mercury* (Leeds, England). Saturday, 18 July, 1818; issue 2775.
50. Georgian Papers Online (http://gpp.rct.uk, October 2019) RA GEO/ ADD/4/134, William, Duke of Clarence, to Sir Richard Puleston, St James's, 15 December 1820.
51. Wellesley, Arthur, 2nd Duke of Wellington (ed.) (1828). *Dispatches, Correspondence and Memoranda of Field Marshal Arthur Duke of Wellington, KG. Vol VII*. London: John Murray, p.9.
52. Ibid., p.93.
53. *The Age* (London, England). Sunday, 27 June 1830.
54. Greville, Charles CG (1875). *The Greville Memoirs: Vol I*. New York: D Appleton and Company, p.361.

55. Ibid., p.362.

56. Tragically, George committed suicide in 1842 after a lengthy struggle with mental illness. He shot himself with a gun that had been a gift from his uncle, George IV.

57. *Bell's Life in London and Sporting Chronicle* (London, England). Sunday, 11 December 1831; issue 507.

58. *Bell's Life in London and Sporting Chronicle* (London, England). Sunday, 19 August 1832; issue 372.

59. Ibid.

60. Claims that Adelaide attributed the ruinous 1834 Palace of Westminster fire to divine vengeance on the reformers were apparently equally apocryphal.

61. Pelham, Camden (1841). *The Chronicles of Crime; or, The New Newgate Calendar, Vol II*. London: Thomas Tegg, p.357.

62. *Morning Chronicle* (London, England). Wednesday, 21 June 1837; issue 21093.

63. Adelaide outlived her husband by twelve years. She died in 1849, aged 57.

Act Five

1. *London Evening Post* (London, England), 3 November 1767–5 November 1767; issue 6242.

2. Aspinall, Arthur (ed.) (1965). *The Correspondence of George, Prince of Wales, Vol I*. Cassell: London, p.32.

3. Neale, Erskine (1850). *The Life of Field-Marshal His Royal Highness, Edward, Duke of Kent*. London: Richard Bentley, p.8.

4. Fisher held a number of offices in the royal household before his appointment first as Bishop of Exeter and later Salisbury, where he remained until his death in 1825. Fisher was also one of the closest friends of the famed John Constable, at whose wedding he officiated.

5. Aspinall, Arthur (ed.) (1966). *The Later Correspondence of George III, Vol. I*. Cambridge: Cambridge University Press, p.129.

6. Ibid., p.207.

7. Ibid., p.239.

8. Ibid., p.323.

9. Ibid., p.324.

10. Georgian Papers Online (http://gpp.rct.uk, October 2019) RA GEO/MAIN/16655, Lieutenant Colonel George von Wangenheim to George III, 6 January 1790.

11. *General Evening Post* (London, England). 14 January 1790–16 January 1790; issue 8775.

12. *Argus* (London, England). Saturday, 16 January 1790; issue 260.

13. Gillen, Mollie (1970). *The Prince and His Lady*. London: Sidgwick & Jackson, p.19.

14. Ibid., p.23.

15. Ibid.
16. Aspinall, Arthur (ed.) (1966). *The Later Correspondence of George III, Vol. I.* Cambridge: Cambridge University Press, p.508.
17. Aspinall, Arthur (ed.) (1791). *The Correspondence of George, Prince of Wales: Vol II.* Oxford: Oxford University Press, p.132.
18. *The Times* (London, England). Friday, 29 July, 1791; issue 2088.
19. The couple were also cousins.
20. Anonymous (1791). *Ancient French Archives or Extracts from the Minutes of Council Relating to the Records of Canada While Under the Government of France.* Quebec: Canada Council, p.45.
21. *General Evening Post* (London, England). 1 November 1798–3 November 1798; issue 10318.
22. *The Times* (London, England). Monday, 29 March 1802; issue 5377.
23. Neale, Erskine (1850). *The Life of Field-Marshal His Royal Highness, Edward, Duke of Kent.* London: Richard Bentley, p.104.
24. *Morning Post* (London, England). Tuesday, 25 January 1803; issue 10705.
25. Aspinall, Arthur (1971). *Aspinall, Arthur. The Correspondence of George, Prince of Wales, Vol IV.* Cambridge: Cambridge University Press, p.357.
26. Ibid., p.359.
27. Ibid., p.360.
28. Ibid., p.366.
29. Georgian Papers Online (http://gpp.rct.uk, October 2019) RA GEO/MAIN/39891, Prince Edward, Duke of Kent and Strathearn, to Prince Frederick, Duke of York and Albany, 6 June 1803.
30. Anderson, William James (1870). *The Life of Field-Marshal His Royal Highness Edward, Duke of Kent.* Ottawa: Hunter, Rose & Company, p.89.
31. Aspinall, Arthur (1968). *The Later Correspondence of George III, Vol V.* Cambridge: Cambridge University Press, p.76.
32. Clarke, Mary Anne (1810). *The Rival Princes, Vol I.* London: David Longworth, pp.114–116.
33. *The Morning Chronicle* (London, England). Saturday, 5 October 1816; issue 14798.
34. *The Morning Chronicle* (London, England). Saturday, 15 February 1817; issue 14912.
35. *Morning Chronicle* (London, England). Thursday, 14 May 1818; issue 15299.
36. *Salisbury and Winchester Chronicle* (Salisbury, England). Sunday, 31 May 1819; issue 4215.
37. *Morning Post* (London, England). Wednesday, 26 January 1820; issue 15295.
38. The duke's stepchildren by his marriage to Victoria, Duchess of Kent, enjoyed distinguished lives. Carl, 3rd Prince of Leiningen, was very briefly prime minister of the German Empire, whilst Princess Feodora of Leiningen married Ernest l, Prince of Hohenlohe-Langenburg, and was a lifelong friend of her half-sister, Queen Victoria.

Bibliography

Abbott, Thomas Eastoe. *The Soldier's Friend; or, Memorials of Brunswick*. Hull: I Wilson, 1828.

Adolphus, John. *Memoirs of John Bannister, Comedian, Vol. I*. London: Richard Bentley, 1839.

Allen, Walter Gore. *King William IV*. London: The Cresset Press, 1960.

Andrews, Jonathan & Scull, Andrew. *Undertaker of the Mind*. Berkeley: University of California Press, 2001.

Anonymous. *Ancient French Archives or Extracts from the Minutes of Council Relating to the Records of Canada While Under the Government of France*. Quebec: Canada Council, 1791.

Anonymous. *Court Life Below Stairs, Vol IV*. London: Hurst and Blackett, 1883.

Anonymous. *George III: His Court and Family, Vol I*. London: Henry Colburn and Co, 1820.

Anonymous. *An Historical Account of the Life and Reign of King George the Fourth*. London: G Smeeton, 1830.

Anonymous. *Leaves from the Diary of an Officer of the Guards*. London: Chapman and Hall, 1854.

Anonymous. *A Letter to Mrs Clarke on her Late Connection with the Duke of York*. London: J Bell, 1809.

Anonymous. *The Memoirs of Perdita*. London: G Lister, 1784.

Anonymous. *The New Jamaica Almanack, and Register, 1801*. Kingston: Stevenson and Aikman, 1801.

Anonymous. *The Parliamentary Debates from the Year 1803 to the Present Time, Volume XXXI*. London: TC Hansard, 1815.

Anonymous. *The Parliamentary History of England from the Earliest Period to the Year 1803, XVII*. London: Longman, Hurst, Rees, Orme, & Brown, 1813.

Anonymous. *The Quarterly Review, Vol. 270*. London: John Murray, 1938.

Anonymous. *The Royal Fusiliers in An Outline of Military History*. Aldershot: Gale & Polden, Ltd, 1926.

Arbuthnot, Harriet. *The Journal of Mrs Arbuthnot, 1820-1832, Vol I*. London: Macmillan, 1950.

Arundel, Theophilus. *Caroline von Linsingen and King William the Fourth*. London: W Swan Sonnenschein & Allen, 1880

Aspinall, Arthur (ed.). *The Correspondence of George, Prince of Wales: Vol I*. Oxford: Oxford University Press, 1971.

Aspinall, Arthur (ed.). *The Correspondence of George, Prince of Wales, Vol II*. Oxford: Oxford University Press, 1971.

Aspinall, Arthur (ed.). *The Correspondence of George, Prince of Wales, Vol II.* London: Cassell, 1963.

Aspinall, Arthur. *The Correspondence of George, Prince of Wales, Vol IV.* Oxford: Oxford University Press, 1971.

Aspinall, Arthur. *The Correspondence of George, Prince of Wales, Vol VI.* Oxford: Oxford University Press, 1971.

Aspinall Arthur (ed.). *Later Correspondence of George III: December 1783 to January 1793.* Cambridge: Cambridge University Press, 1920.

Aspinall, Arthur (ed.). *The Later Correspondence of George III, Vol. I.* Cambridge: Cambridge University Press, 1966.

Aspinall, Arthur. *The Later Correspondence of George III, Vol II.* Cambridge: Cambridge University Press, 1962.

Aspinall, Arthur. *The Later Correspondence of George III, Vol III.* Cambridge: Cambridge University Press, 1963.

Aspinall, Arthur. *The Later Correspondence of George III, Vol IV.* Cambridge: Cambridge University Press, 1968.

Aspinall, Arthur. *The Later Correspondence of George III, Vol V.* Cambridge: Cambridge University Press, 1970.

Aspinall, Arthur (ed.). *Letters of the Princess Charlotte, 1811-1817.* London: Home and Van Thal, 1949.

Aspinall, Arthur (ed.). *Mrs Jordan and Her Family: Being the Unpublished Correspondence of Mrs Jordan and the Duke of Clarence, Later William IV.* London: Arthur Barker, 1951.

Beatty, Michael A. *The English Royal Family of America, from Jamestown to the American Revolution.* Jefferson: McFarland & Company, Inc, 2003.

Black, Jeremy. *George III: America's Last King.* New Haven: Yale University Press, 2008.

Black, Jeremy. *The Hanoverians: The History of a Dynasty.* London: Hambledon and London, 2007.

Boaden, James. *The Life of Mrs Jordan, Vol I.* London: Edward Bull, 1831.

Boaden, James. *The Life of Mrs Jordan, Vol II.* London: Edward Bull, 1831.

Bury, Lady Charlotte Campbell. *Diary Illustrative of the Times of George the Fourth, Vol. I.* London: Henry Colburn, 1839.

Bury, Lady Charlotte Campbell. *Diary Illustrative of the Times of George the Fourth: Vol II.* London: Carey, Lea and Blanchard, 1838.

Bury, Lady Charlotte Campbell. *Diary Illustrative of the Times of George the Fourth: Vol III.* London: Henry Colburn, 1839.

Bury, Lady Charlotte Campbell. *The Murdered Queen!.* London: W Emans, 1838.

Byrne, Paula. *Perdita: The Life of Mary Robinson.* London: Harper Press, 2012.

Catania, Steven, "Brandy Nan and Farmer George: Public Perceptions of Royal Health and the Demystification of English Monarchy During the Long Eighteenth Century" (2014). *Dissertations.* Paper 1255. http://ecommons.luc.edu/luc_diss/1255

Chapman, Hester W. *Privileged Persons.* London: Reynal & Hitchcock, 1966.

Clarke, Mary Anne. *Biographical Memoirs & Anecdotes of the Celebrated Mrs Clarke.* London: W Wilson, 1809.

Clarke, Mary Anne. *A Letter Addressed to the Right Honourable William Fitzgerald.* London: J Williams, 1813.

Clarke, Mary Anne. *Minutes of Evidence: Authentic and Interesting Memoirs of Mrs Clarke.* London: C Chapple, 1809.

Clarke, Mary Anne. *The Rival Princes.* New York: David Longworth, 1810.

Clarke, ML, "The Education of Royalty in the Eighteenth Century: George IV and William IV." *British Journal of Educational Studies*, vol. 26, no. 1, 1978, pp. 73–87. *JSTOR*, www.jstor.org/stable/3120477.

Clarke, W. *The Authentic and Impartial Life of Mrs. Mary Anne Clarke.* London: T Kelly, 1809.

Cole, Hubert. *Beau Brummell.* London: HarperCollins Distribution Services, 1977.

Craig, William Marshall. *Memoir of Her Majesty Sophia Charlotte of Mecklenburg Strelitz, Queen of Great Britain.* Liverpool: Henry Fisher, 1818.

Curzon, Catherine. *Kings of Georgian Britain.* Barnsley: Pen & Sword, 2017.

Curzon, Catherine. *Queens of Georgian Britain.* Barnsley: Pen & Sword, 2017.

Curzon, Catherine. *The Scandal of George III's Court.* Barnsley: Pen & Sword, 2018.

David, Saul. *Prince of Pleasure.* New York: Grove Press, 2000.

Delves Broughton, Vernon (ed.). *Court and Private Life in the Time of Queen Charlotte.* London: Richard Bentley, 1887.

Dickenson, Mary Hamilton. *Mary Hamilton: Afterwards Mrs. John Dickenson, at Court and at Home.* London: John Murray, 1925.

Donne, Bodham W (ed.). *The Correspondence of King George the Third With Lord North from 1768 to 1783: Vol I.* London: John Murray, 1867.

Fitzgerald, Percy. *The Good Queen Charlotte.* London: Downey & Co, 1899.

Fitzgerald, Percy. *The Life and Times of William IV, Vol I.* London: Tinsley Brothers, 1884.

Fitzgerald, Percy. *The Life and Times of William IV, Vol II.* London: Tinsley Brothers, 1884.

Fitzgerald, Percy. *The Royal Dukes and Princesses of the Family of George III, Vol I.* London: Tinsley Brothers, 1882.

Fitzgerald, Percy. *The Royal Dukes and Princesses of the Family of George III, Vol II.* London: Tinsley Brothers, 1882.

Gillen, Mollie. *The Prince and His Lady.* London: Sidgwick & Jackson, 1970.

Glenbervie, Sylvester Douglas. *The Diaries of Sylvester Douglas, Lord Glenbervie.* London: Constable & Co Ltd, 1928.

Glover, Richard. *Peninsular Preparation: The Reform of the British Army 1795–1809.* Cambridge: Cambridge University Press, 1963.

Gore, John (ed.). *Creevey's Life and times.* London: John Murray, 1934.

Greville, Charles CG. *The Greville Memoirs: Vol I.* New York: D Appleton and Company, 1875.

Gronow, Rees Howell. *Reminiscences of Captain Gronow.* London: Smith, Elder and Co., 1862.

Hadlow, Janice. *The Strangest Family: The Private Lives of George III, Queen Charlotte and the Hanoverians*. London: William Collins, 2014.

Haggard, John. *Reports of Cases Argued and Determined in the Ecclesiastical Courts at Doctor's Commons, and in the High Court of Delegates, Vol I*. London: W Benning, 1829.

Hague, William. *William Pitt the Younger*. London: Harper Perennial, 2005.

Hamilton, Richard Vesey (ed.). *Letters and Papers of Admiral of the Fleet Sir Thos. Byam Martin, Vol I, 1903*. Navy Records Society: London, 1903.

Harcourt, Leveson Vernon (ed.). *The Diaries and Correspondence of the Right Hon. George Rose, Vol II*. London: Richard Bentley, 1860.

Heard, Kate. *High Spirits: The Comic Art of Thomas Rowlandson*. London: Royal Collection Trust, 2013.

Hedley, Owen. *Queen Charlotte*. London: J Murray, 1975.

Hibbert, Christopher. *George III: A Personal History*. London: Viking, 1998.

Hibbert, Christopher. *George IV*. London: Penguin, 1976.

Hogan, Denis. *An Appeal to the Public, and a Farewell Address to the Army*. London: G Gorman, 1808.

Holt, Edward. *The Public and Domestic Life of His Late Most Gracious Majesty, George the Third, Vol I*. London: Sherwood, Neely and Jones, 1820.

Holt, Edward. *The Public and Domestic Life of His Late Most Gracious Majesty, George the Third, Vol II*. London: Sherwood, Neely and Jones, 1820.

Huish, Robert. *Authentic Memoir of His Late Royal Highness Frederick Duke of York and Albany*. London: John Williams, 1827.

Huish, Robert. *The History of the Life and Reign of William the Fourth*. London: William Emans, 1837.

Huish, Robert. *Memoirs of George the Fourth, Vol I*. London: T Kelly, 1830.

Huish, Robert. *Memoirs of Her Late Majesty Caroline, Queen of Great Britain*. London: T Kelly, 1821.

Irvine, Valerie. *The King's Wife: George IV and Mrs Fitzherbert*. London: Hambledon, 2007.

Jeffrey, Reginald (ed.). *Dyott's Diary 1781-1845: Vol I*. London: Archibald Constable and Company, Ltd, 1907.

Jerrold, Clare. *The Story of Dorothy Jordan*. London: Eveleigh Nash, 1914.

Jesse Heneage, J. *Memoirs of the Life and Reign of King George the Third, Vol II*. London: Tinsley Brothers, 1867.

Jesse Heneage, J. *Memoirs of the Life and Reign of King George the Third, Vol III*. London: Richard Bentley, 1843.

Jesse Heneage, J. *Memoirs of the Life and Reign of King George the Third, Vol IV*. Boston, LC Page & Company, 1902.

Kiste, John van der. *George III's Children*. Stroud: The History Press, 2004.

Langdale, Charles. *Memoirs of Mrs. Fitzherbert*. London: Richard Bentley, 1856.

Leslie, Anita. *Mrs Fitzherbert: A Biography*. York: Scribner, 1960.

Leslie, Shane. *Mrs. Fitzherbert: A Life Chiefly from Unpublished Sources*. New York: Benziger Brothers, 1939.

Lloyd, Hannibal Evans. *George IV: Memoirs of His Life and Reign, Interspersed with Numerous Personal Anecdotes*. London: Treuttel and Würtz, 1830.

Marsh, Charles. *The Clubs of London: Vol I*. London: Henry Colburn and Richard Bentley, 1832.

Melville, Lewis. *Farmer George, Vol I*. London: Sir Isaac Pitman and Sons, Ltd, 1907.

Minto, Emma Eleanor Elizabeth (ed.). *Life and Letters of Sir Gilbert Elliot First Earl of Minto from 1751 to 1806, Vol I*. London: Longmans, Green, and Company, 1874.

Musteen, Jason R. *Nelson's Refuge*. Annapolis: Naval Institute Press, 2011.

Naftel, William D. *Prince Edward's Legacy*. Halifax: Formac Publishing Company, 2005

Neale, Erskine. *The Life of Field-Marshal His Royal Highness, Edward, Duke of Kent*. London: Richard Bentley, 1850.

Oulton, CW. *Authentic and Impartial Memoirs of Her Late Majesty: Charlotte Queen of Great Britain and Ireland*. London: J Robins and Co, 1818.

Pelham, Camden (1841). *The Chronicles of Crime; or, The New Newgate Calendar, Vol II*. London: Thomas Tegg, 1841.

Peters, TJ & Beveridge, A, "The Blindness, Deafness and Madness of King George III: Psychiatric Interactions" (2010). *The Journal of the Royal College of Physicians of Edinburgh*, Vol 40: issue 1. https://www.rcpe.ac.uk/sites/default/files/peters_1.pdf

Robins, Jane. *The Trial of Queen Caroline: The Scandalous Affair that Nearly Ended a Monarchy*. New York: Simon and Schuster, 2006.

Ronald, DAB. *Young Nelsons*. London: Osprey Publishing, 2012.

Rushton, Alan R. *Royal Maladies*. Victoria: Trafford Publishing, 2008.

Smith, EA. *George IV*. New Haven: Yale University Press, 1999.

Smith, William James (ed.). *The Greville Papers: Vol III*. London: John Murray, 1853.

Taylor, Ernest (ed.). *The Taylor Papers*. London: Longmans, Green, and Co, 1913.

Thackeray, William Makepeace. *The Works of William Makepeace Thackeray: Vol XIX*. London: Smith, Elder, & Co, 1869.

Tidridge, Nathan. *Prince Edward, Duke of Kent*. Dundurn: Toronto, 2013.

Tillyard, Stella. *A Royal Affair: George III and his Troublesome Siblings*. London: Vintage, 2007.

Tomalin, Claire. *Mrs Jordan's Profession*. London: Penguin, 2003.

Urban, Sylvanus. *The Gentleman's Magazine: and Historical Chronicle, Volume XCVII*. London: John Harris, 1827.

Walpole, Horace. *The Last Journals of Horace Walpole During the Reign of George III from 1771–1783*. London: John Lane, 1910.

Walpole, Horace. *Letters of Horace Walpole, Earl of Orford to Sir Horace Mann*. London: Richard Bentley, 1833.

Walpole, Horace. *Letters of Horace Walpole, Earl of Orford, to Sir Horace Mann, Vol I*. London: Richard Bentley, 1843.

Walpole, Horace. *Letters of Horace Walpole, Earl of Orford to Sir Horace Mann, Vol II*. Philadelphia: Lea & Blanchard, 1844.

Walpole, Horace. *Letters of Horace Walpole, Earl of Orford to Sir Horace Mann, Vol III*. London: Richard Bentley, 1833.

Walpole, Horace. *Letters of Horace Walpole, Earl of Orford to Sir Horace Mann, Vol IV*. London: Richard Bentley, 1844.

Walpole, Horace. *The Letters of Horace Walpole: Vol I*. London: Lea and Blanchard, 1842.

Walpole, Horace. *The Letters of Horace Walpole: Vol II*. New York: Dearborn, 1832.

Walpole, Horace. *Memoirs of the Reign of King George the Third: Vol I*. Philadelphia: Lea & Blanchard, 1845.

Walpole, Horace. *Memoirs of the Reign of King George the Third: Vol II*. Philadelphia: Lea & Blanchard, 1845.

Walpole, Horace. *Memoirs of the Reign of King George the Third: Vol III*. London: Richard Bentley, 1845.

Walpole, Horace. *Memoirs of the Reign of King George the Third: Vol IV*. London: Richard Bentley, 1845.

Walpole, Horace and Doran, John (ed.). *Journal of the Reign of King George the Third, Vol I*. London, Richard Bentley, 1859.

Walpole, Horace and Doran, John (ed.). *Journal of the Reign of King George the Third, Vol II*. London, Richard Bentley, 1859.

Watkins, John. *A Biographical Memoir of His Late Royal Highness Frederick, Duke of York and Albany*. London: Henry Fisher, Son, and Co, 1827.

Watkins, John. *The Life and Times of William the Fourth*. London: Fisher, Son, and Jackson, 1831.

Watkins, John. *Memoirs of Her Most Excellent Majesty Sophia-Charlotte, Queen of Great Britain*. London: Richard Bentley, 1845.

Wellesley, Arthur, 2nd Duke of Wellington (ed.). *Dispatches, Correspondence and Memoranda of Field Marshal Arthur Duke of Wellington, KG. Vol VII*. London: John Murray, 1828.

Williams, Thomas. *Memoirs of Her Late Majesty Queen Charlotte*. London: W Simpkin and R Marshall, 1819.

Williams, Thomas. *Memoirs of His Late Majesty George III*. London: W Simpkin and R Marshall, 1820.

Winterbottom, Derek. *The Grand Old Duke of York*. Barnsley: Pen and Sword, 2016.

Wraxall, Nathaniel (1836). *Posthumous Memoirs of His Own Time, Vol III*. London: Richard Bentley, 1836.

Newspapers

The Age (London, England). Sunday, 27 June 1830.

Argus (London, England). Saturday, 16 January 1790; issue 260.

Bell's Life in London and Sporting Chronicle (London, England). Sunday, 19 August 1832; issue 372.

Bell's Life in London and Sporting Chronicle (London, England). Sunday, 11 December 1831; issue 507.

Evening Mail (London, England). 31 October–2 November 1791; issue 419.

The Examiner (London, England), Sunday, 27 June 1830; issue 1139.

Freeman's Journal or The North American Intelligencer (London, England), Wednesday, 23 January 1782; issue 40.

Gazetteer and London Daily Advertiser (London, England), Friday, 13 August 1762; issue 10392.

Gazetteer and London Daily Advertiser (London, England), Wednesday, 17 August 1763; issue 10742.

Gazetteer and New Daily Advertiser (London, England), Monday, 26 August 1765; issue 11374.

General Evening Post (London, England). 14 January 1790–16 January 1790; issue 8775.

General Evening Post (London, England). 1 November 1798–3 November 1798; issue 10318.

Glasgow Herald (Glasgow, Scotland). 30 June 1820; issue 1828

Hull Packet (Hull, England). Tuesday, 16 July 1816; issue 1551.

Lancaster Gazetter (Lancaster, England), Saturday, 16 February 1811; issue 505.

Leeds Mercury (Leeds, England). Saturday, 18 July 1818; issue 2775.

London Evening Post (London, England), 10 August 1762–12 August 1762; issue 5422.

London Evening Post (London, England), 3 November 1767–5 November 1767; issue 6242.

London Gazette (London, England), 27 September 1791–1 October 1791; issue 13347.

Morning Chronicle (London, England). Saturday, 20 February 1813; issue 13664.

The Morning Chronicle (London, England). Saturday, 15 February 1817; issue 14912.

The Morning Chronicle (London, England). Saturday, 5 October 1816; issue 14798.

Morning Chronicle (London, England), Friday, 7 November 1817; issue 15138.

Morning Chronicle (London, England). Thursday, 14 May 1818; issue 15299.

Morning Chronicle (London, England), Monday, 7 August 1820; issue 15999.

Morning Chronicle (London, England). Wednesday, 21 June 1837; issue 21093.

Morning Post (London, England). Wednesday, 19 October 1791; issue 5768.

Morning Post (London, England). Tuesday, 25 January 1803; issue 10705.

Morning Post (London, England). Saturday, 11 October 1806; issue 11124.

Morning Post (London, England), Friday, 3 February 1809; issue 11863.

Morning Post (London, England). Wednesday, 26 January 1820; issue 15295.

Morning Post (London, England), Friday, 21 January 1820; issue 15299.

Morning Post (London, England), Wednesday, 16 August 1820; issue 15418.

Morning Star (London, England), Thursday, 28 May 1789; issue 91.

Northampton Mercury (Northampton, England), Saturday 22 October 1791; issue 33.

Northampton Mercury (Northampton, England), Saturday, 18 March 1809; issue 2.

The Reading Mercury and Oxford Gazette, etc (Reading, England). Monday, 26 January 1789; issue 1410.

The Salisbury and Winchester Journal (Salisbury, England), Monday, 18 February 1788; issue 2593.

Salisbury and Winchester Chronicle (Salisbury, England). Sunday, 31 May 1819; issue 4215.

St. James's Chronicle or the British Evening Post (London, England), 4 October 1791–6 October 1791; issue 4673.

The Telegraph (London, England), Tuesday, 30 December 1794, issue 1.

The Times (London, England), Wednesday, 3 December 1788, issue 1187.

The Times (London, England). Saturday, 24 January 1789; issue 1230.

The Times (London, England). Friday, 29 July 1791; issue 2088.

The Times (London, England). Thursday, 13 October 1791; issue 2152.

The Times (London: England). Tuesday, 29 November 1791; issue 2193.

The Times (London, England), Saturday, 9 January 1796; issue 3487.

The Times (London, England). Monday 29 March 1802; issue 5377.

The Times (London, England). Thursday, 12 December 1811; issue 8471.

The Times (London, England), Monday, 6 May 1816; issue 9827.

The Times (London, England), Wednesday, 7 June 1820; issue 10953.

The Times (London, England), Monday, 7 August 1820; issue 11005.

Whitehall Evening Post (1770) (London, England). 12 October 1780–14 October 1780.

Websites Consulted

British History Online (http://www.british-history.ac.uk)

British Newspapers 1600–1950 (http://gdc.gale.com/products/19thcentury british-library-newspapers-part-i-and-part-ii/)

Georgian Papers Online (https://gpp.royalcollection.org.uk), Royal Archives, Windsor

Hansard (http://hansard.millbanksystems.com/index.html)

Historical Texts (http://historicaltexts.jisc.ac.uk)

House of Commons Parliamentary Papers (http://parlipapers.chadwyck. co.uk/marketing/index.jsp)

JSTOR (www.jstor.org)

The National Archives (http://www.nationalarchives.gov.uk)

Oxford Dictionary of National Biography (http://www.oxforddnb.com)

Queen Victoria's Journals (http://www.queenvictoriasjournals.org)

State Papers Online (https://www.gale.com/intl/primary-sources/statepapers-online)

The Times Digital Archive (http://gale.cengage.co.uk/times-digitalarchive/times-digital-archive-17852006.aspx)

Index